T0195806

science education *for* **gifted students**

a
G͏IFTED C͏HILD T͏ODAY *reader*

science education
for gifted students

edited by
susan k. johnsen
and
james kendrick

Routledge
Taylor & Francis Group

NEW YORK AND LONDON

First published 2005 by Prufrock Press Inc.

Published 2021 by Routledge
605 Third Avenue, New York, NY 10017
2 Park Square, Milton Park, Abingdon, Oxon OX14 4RN

Routledge is an imprint of the Taylor & Francis Group, an informa business

Library of Congress Cataloging-in-Publication Data

Science education for gifted students /
edited by Susan K. Johnsen and James Kendrick.
        p. cm. — (A Gifted child today reader)
    Includes bibliographical references.
    ISBN 1-59363-167-7
    1. Science—Study and teaching. 2. Gifted children—Identification. 3.
Gidted children—Education. I. Johnsen, Susan K. II. Kendrick, James,
1974– III. Series.

    Q181.S3688 2005
    371.95'335—dc22
                                                            2005018785

ISBN 13: 978-1-59363-167-3 (pbk)

Contents

Section III
Science Units for Gifted Students

Overview

hese articles from *Gifted Child Today* and *The Journal of Secondary Gifted Education* were selected specifically for the teacher who is searching for ways to serve students who are gifted in science. This overview provides a brief summary of the authors' major concepts covered in each of the chapters, including (a) characteristics of students who are gifted in science, (b) identification of students gifted in science, (c) qualities of teachers who are effective in working with these gifted students, (d) attributes of a differentiated science curriculum, and (e) model units for teaching gifted students in science classrooms.

Students who are gifted in science know many varied facts, understand scientific concepts in depth (Gould, Weeks, & Evans), and are insightful in transferring learning from specific examples to a whole class of such examples (Ngoi & Vodracek). They gain this knowledge by closely observing things around them (Karnes & Riley), identifying problems that others may miss (Meador), experimenting with ideas, and actually enjoying the pleasure of not knowing the answer (Karnes & Riley). They are passionate about science, as indicated by motivation, persistence, inventiveness, and natural curiosity (Karnes & Riley). They also tend to excel in mathematics (Gould, Weeks, & Evans; Ngoi & Vondracek). Some students who are gifted in science, however, may experience difficulty with reading, writing, and organizational skills (Cooper, Baum, & Neu). To develop their talents, these students need a more active, hands-on engagement in scientific activities.

In identifying students who are gifted in science, Ngoi and Vodracek suggest a more informal approach in which the teacher keeps anecdotal records and notes which students not only master concepts quickly, but also demonstrate scientific insight (the ability to make connections between concepts). They believe that high scores on tests do not necessarily identify gifted students in this domain. Similar to Ngoi and Vodracek, Cooper, Baum, and Neu also rely on observations in the identification process. Their Talent Discovery Assessment Process uses trained observers to record behaviors of students who are engaged in planned scientific activities associated with a variety of domains, including biological and physical science.

The teachers who are most effective when working with these gifted students assume more facilitative, mentoring roles (Mackin, Macaroglu, & Russell; Menelly). Robinson recommends that teachers be involved in their own scientific research, participate in expeditions, and immerse themselves in the language of science and research. These expeditions may be in exotic locations, close to home, or even virtual. He believes that this type of personal involvement helps the teacher renew enthusiasm for the subject and develop student activities that are more hands-on.

A differentiated curriculum needs to be organized around basic scientific principles that require more advanced levels of thinking, complex processes, and creative products (Cooper, Baum, & Neu; Gould, Weeks, & Evans; Meador). The content is accelerated using concepts from above-average grade levels (Gould, Weeks, & Evans) and courses that combine domains (e.g., chemistry and physics) and concepts from high school and college levels (Ngoi & Vondracek). Enrichment occurs through the use of authentic, professional activities (White), after-school projects (Mennelly), and competitions (Gould, Weeks, & Evans; Karnes & Riley; Ngoi & Vondracek).

Highly recommended instructional strategies incorporate hands-on experimentation and original research. At the primary level, Meador suggests placing interesting objects from nature in the classroom to encourage questioning and to engage students in specific scientific processes such as observing, classifying, predicting, comparing, hypothesizing, defining, and controlling variables. Older students will want to become more involved in their own research, which may be supported by a mentor from the high school or university level (Ngoi & Vondracek). This research might be conducted within an elective course or seminar for credit, as an outgrowth of a special interest, or as an extracurricular activity in an academic competition or an after-school enrichment laboratory (Karnes & Riley; Mackin, Macroglu, & Russell; Mennelly; Ngoi & Vondracek). In all cases, the teacher moves the student through stages of talent development from novice to expert (Cooper, Baum, & Neu). These stages include the students' becoming initially excited about the topic, learning the skills to find and pursue problems independently, and sharing their research with others.

Some of the authors provide units of study and specific lessons that model best practices in teaching science. In Mennelly's unit, "The Atomic Relay," he integrates science with physical education to teach a basic understanding of atomic structure and electrons. Budd uses hands-on activities to help students understand how magnetism is used to levitate a vehicle. Students explore principles and then design, construct, test, and evaluate their own Maglev vehicles. White uses a real archaeological site—an empty lot of a recently razed structure—to teach scientific processes. His students form a working hypothesis, observe the physical site, grid the site, maintain formal field records, label and catalogue artifacts, produce a site report, and ultimately create a museum display.

We want to thank these authors for their contributions. We hope this book assists you in teaching students who are gifted in science.

Susan K. Johnsen
James Kendrick
Editors

section one

Science in the Primary Years

chapter 1

Science Starts Early

*a program for developing
talent in science*

by **J. Christine Gould, Valerie Weeks,**
and **Sarah Evans**

t the age of 4, Jacob announced to his teacher, "When I grow up, I'm going to be a oceanographer or . . . a squid . . . 'cause they're scary and they squirt black ink at everyone! Then I can squirt black ink at you, but you can't squirt black ink at me!"

Although becoming either an oceanographer or a squid seemed noble goals, his Early Childhood Accelerated Program (ECAP*R) teacher, Valerie Weeks, began to wonder what would happen if science was presented to young, potentially gifted children in a developmentally appropriate way. Although no longer active, the ECAP*R program (Gould, Thorpe, & Weeks, 2001), which was located in Wichita, Kansas, served potentially gifted children 3–5 years in age with a wide range of abilities and needs. During its years of operation, the ECAP*R program provided an important niche for children whose parents were unable to find challenging, but developmentally appropriate preschool programs for them.

Jacob was one of those students. He had been asked to leave two different preschool settings due to behavioral problems such as bickering, fighting, and shoving other children. At the same time, though, Jacob showed several indicators of early giftedness (Davis & Rimm, 1998; Piirto,1999). For example, he knew many varied facts about the ocean and the creatures that live in it. He could complete fairly complex math problems in his head. He read at the fourth-grade level. Jacob's last teacher suggested to his mother that he might have Attention-Deficit Hyperactivity Disorder (ADHD). Soon after, he was evaluated and accepted into the ECAP*R program, where he was introduced to a curriculum that was sensitive to his level of development and his need for mental stimulation. Jacob's behavioral problems didn't disappear; he still had difficulty with interpersonal relationships. However, they were moderated, and it became clear that he was simply an active little boy who needed the right kind of mental stimulation. Without the types of experiences that a program like ECAP*R provides to meet Jacob's developmental and intellectual needs, he could possibly remain "at risk" for school and social failure. He is not alone.

Jacob's future career aspirations became the impetus for "Science Starts Early," which was developed by Valerie Weeks, ECAP*R program coordinator, teacher, and cofounder, in collaboration with Sarah Evans, assistant professor of biology at Friends University in Wichita, Kansas. The intent was to expose young, potentially gifted children to basic scientific principles that would allow them to explore the world around them. Active learning and experimentation became two foundational elements of the program. Developmentally appropriate critical thinking that leads to incisive questioning became the third.

This chapter describes the Science Starts Early program and how it effectively got young children—as young as age 3—interested in scientific concepts, starting them on their way to a lifetime of studying science. This is particularly important because many students avoid science and math because of negative early exposures. Thus, teachers of young children need to take extra steps to ensure that their gifted students see the fun and wonder science can offer.

Attitudes Toward Science

In her work at Friends University, Dr. Evans teaches two groups of adult learners. The first group of students is composed of nonscience majors. At the beginning of each semester, Dr. Evans informally interviews each member of the class. She asks two questions: "What kind of science background do you have?" and "What are your future goals?" Over the last several years, a consistent majority of the students have indicated that they had negative experiences in science classes as far back as elementary school. These same students usually added that they were taking science now because it was a requirement and they found science difficult and boring. As for their future plans, they wished to become accountants, managers, Web designers, or members of another profession not related to science. Of more concern is the frequently verbalized idea that they couldn't pursue a profession because it might require a science background. They saw themselves as incapable.

The second group of students is composed of biology and chemistry majors. Dr. Evans also conducts an informal interview with each of these students at the beginning of the semester and asks the same questions, but receives far different responses. These students consistently answer that they have had positive experiences with science that got them interested in becoming researchers, physicians, environmental scientists, naturalists, and even zoo keepers. The prevailing negative feeling toward science does not seem to be present with this group of students.

What is the cause of the attitudinal differences these two groups have toward the study of science? Over the past decade, research related to this area has focused on adolescent girls and, to a lesser extent, all students and two school subjects many students avoid: science and mathematics. Relevant literature was distilled in the 1992 report conducted by the American Association of University Women entitled *How Schools Shortchange Girls: A Study of Major Findings on Girls and Education*. This report found that there may be a complex interaction of social reasons that explain why some students don't pursue the study of science; these include lack of confidence, relevance of science, differences in play experiences, stereotypes about who takes science, and lack of support for persisting in the study of scientific areas. The report concluded,

> In general, students' interest in and enthusiasm for math and science decline the longer they are in school . . . most students who dislike science say science is "not interesting." Adolescent girls are more likely than adolescent boys to find science uninteresting. Adolescent boys are more likely than girls to discount the importance of science itself. (p. 30)

However, other reasons may also be factors. The way science has traditionally been taught in schools, especially in secondary schools, may be unappealing to some students. A competitive classroom atmosphere involving informational lectures followed by paper-pencil tests may not create personal investment in the subject. A lack of personal investment may then lead some students, especially girls, to find science boring (Baker & Leary, 1995; Joyce & Farenga, 2000; Rop, 1997; Schweigardt, Worrell, & Hale, 2001).

The ramifications of not pursuing science at early ages may alter a student's career path in unexpected ways. A student who opts out of science in middle school may later find that there isn't time in his or her school schedule to take all the science needed for admission to selective college programs. The lack of an appropriate science background may result in not being admitted to a medical major or the loss of the opportunity to become an anthropologist or a paleontologist.

The children admitted to the ECAP*R program have advanced abilities and may be representative of those who will impact the scientific future of this country. Because of their potential, another goal of Science Starts Early is to plant a seed of inquiry among very young children—especially girls—that will hopefully continue throughout their lifetimes.

The Science Starts Early Curriculum

Science curricula for children in the early learning stages, although rare, are available. Lucia French of the University of

Rochester developed a program specifically for preschool children entitled ScienceStart! (Jacobson, 2002). It is based on the assumption that children are instinctively curious and interested in how things work. Wanting to understand the ways things work and curiosity about the surrounding world are important qualities for participating in the process of scientific inquiry.

Science Starts Early took advantage of this natural curiosity, which may be more pronounced in potentially gifted children. To create the Science Starts Early curriculum, Mrs. Weeks and Dr. Evans decided on the curriculum together by selecting scientific concepts to be studied. Science textbooks designed for older elementary children through the fifth grade served as important references in the selection process. The other concepts selected for study came from questions verbalized by the children. For example, one day, a girl named Lauren demanded, "Mrs. Weeks, tell us about the black holes in space. I want to know all about black holes in space." That interchange led to a multiweek unit studying the planets and the universe.

In this school/university partnership, Mrs. Weeks laid the foundation and Dr. Evans provided hands-on science experiences. Two to three times each week, Mrs. Weeks prepared the children by teaching the vocabulary needed to discuss a scientific concept. After teaching the appropriate vocabulary, she then began to expose the children to a scientific concept by asking questions about the world around them.

Hypothesize and Experiment

Approximately once every 2 weeks, Dr. Evans visited the classroom and involved the children in an experiment. At one point, they studied "Things That Sink and Things That Float." After a demonstration, children found an object in the room from the many they play with during the day (although the classroom gerbil was placed off-limits). Once the objects were selected, the children came together in a circle to hypothesize about their items and conduct the experiment (see Figure 1.1).

Dr. Evans asked the children to hypothesize whether the item would sink or float. With Jacob's intense interest in oceanography, he was particularly good at this, so he helped the other children—whether they wanted him to or not. During

Introduction
- Discuss the concept to be the subject of today's experiment.
- Discuss why an object might sink or float.

Demonstration 1
- Show the students a round piece of modeling clay.
- Ask the students to hypothesize what will happen when it is placed in a beaker of water.
- Place a round piece of modeling clay into a beaker of water.
- Observe as the clay sinks to the bottom of the beaker.
- Discuss why the clay sank.

Demonstration 2
- Take same piece of modeling clay and shape it into a saucer.
- Ask the students to hypothesize whether it will sink or float.
- Place the clay in the water.
- Observe as the clay floats on the water.
- Discuss the difference in shape between the ball and the saucer.
- Discuss the concept of an air pocket and creation of hollow space.
- Discuss weight, shape, and other characteristics of the clay that caused it to float.

Demonstration 3
- Using the same clay shape as in Demonstration #2, ask the students to hypothesize what will happen when the clay saucer, now floating, is filled with water.
- Fill the clay saucer with water.
- Observe as the clay sinks to the bottom of the beaker.
- Discuss why this happened.
- Discuss the characteristics of the clay that caused it to sink and the differences between the saucer being filled with air or filled with water.
- Discuss why the clay sank and the characteristics of the clay that caused it to sink.

Experiment
- Have the students choose an object from the classroom.
- Student shows the class the chosen object.
- Discuss the characteristics of the object that might determine if it sinks or floats (shape, weight, materials that it is made of).
- Hypothesize whether the object will float or sink in water.
- Student places object in water.
- Class makes observations.
- Discuss the observations, whether the hypothesis was correct, and why.
- Each student has a chance to show their chosen object to the class and put it in water to see if their hypothesis was correct.
- Have the students complete the experiment with the items they have chosen.

Figure 1.1. **Sample experiment:**
Things that sink and things that float

each session, the experimental process continued with other topics. To date, the children have studied chemical reactions, solubility, microbes, invertebrates, density, paper chromatography, and volcanoes. Still to come are magnetism, friction, and properties of light.

For the study of invertebrates, Dr. Evans brought in a microscope with a monitor so everyone could look at a sample of pond water at the same time. Maggie, age 5, found this particularly interesting. She insisted that she be allowed to come up to the front of the room and point out all the creatures moving around so that no one else would miss seeing them. She particularly liked it when an organism was eating or digesting its food, and she wanted to give the organism part of her lunch. Steven, 3 years old, was fascinated by the process of viewing the invertebrates, but became upset when he realized that what he was viewing through the microscope wasn't a video because he had wanted to take the video home to show his whole family.

Invention Convention

Each year, the young scientists shared their new knowledge with other children and guests at an Invention Convention. Each young scientist created an invention and prepared it for an exhibit. Once the young scientist developed an idea, the parents helped him or her prepare the invention and took pictures of each step during the process. The pictures were then attached to a poster board forming an exhibit. The parent helped the child write an explanation of each step of the invention's creation, which was also attached to the poster board. Children from the surrounding area were invited to view the Invention Convention, where the young scientists explained their inventions to anyone who stopped at their poster exhibit. Professors and students from a nearby university judged the exhibits.

Each year, the young scientists invented clever, useful things. One young boy created a cane for his grandmother that had a double use. After having her hip replaced, his grandmother needed support to walk. The young inventor simplified her convalescence by attaching a pillbox to the bottom of her cane, which meant that his grandmother no longer had to carry around extra bottles of pills and, more importantly, she would-n't be able to forget them. One young girl added a bell to her family's entry door for the family cat to ring. Thus, the cat no longer needed to claw at the door, but could announce its presence by ringing the bell with its paw—a very dignified solution to a common problem. Another young boy created something guaranteed to make his father's life much easier: He invented a Plexiglas cover to protect the pages of a book from water so his father could read while in the shower.

At the end of the convention, all the young scientists received prizes awarded by the judges. They all got to explain their inventions to the judges and received positive feedback that encouraged them to keep inventing.

Final Thoughts

Through Science Starts Early, Mrs. Weeks found that the children understood and related to science concepts much better than she had anticipated when the program first started. She was surprised at how much information they retained and how well they seemed to understand science concepts in depth. Their level of understanding was made clear to her during the study of black holes brought about by Lauren's question. The children learned that some scientists think the sun is expected to burn out in approximately 5,000 years. Mrs. Weeks didn't think the children had any concept of a 5,000-year time frame. However, when one child appeared worried about the possibility that the sun might burn out and what would happen to him and his pet frog, several other children replied that 5,000 years was "a long, long time away, so don't worry about it." The problem was solved.

Science Starts Early proved to be a winning program at ECAP*R, and it generated a great deal of interest among the children. After spending several months hypothesizing and experimenting, Jacob was more certain than ever that he wanted to be a form of sea life, most likely a squid—just as long as he was the scariest. Maggie still wanted to see microbes eating their lunch. Steven hoped all the science projects were made into a video. Mrs. Weeks and Dr. Evans hoped they had helped the children form a lasting interest in science. The children in the ECAP*R program were all in agreement: Science that starts early is fun.

References

American Association of University Women. (1992). *How schools shortchange girls: A study of major findings on girls and education.* Washington, DC: American Association of University Women Educational Foundation.

Baker, D., & Leary, R. (1995). Letting girls speak out about science. *Journal of Research in Science Teaching, 32*(1), 3–27.

Davis, G. A., & Rimm, S. B. (1998). *Education of the gifted and talented* (4th ed.). Boston: Allyn and Bacon.

Gould, J. C., Thorpe, P., & Weeks, V. (2001). An early childhood accelerated program. *Educational Leadership, 59*(3), 47–50.

Jacobson, L. (2002). The little scientists. *Education Week on the Web.* Retrieved September 28, 2004, from http://www.edweek.org/ew/newstory.cfm?slug=33preschool.h21

Joyce, B. A., & Farenga, S. J. (2000). Young girls in science: Academic ability, perceptions, and future participation in science. *Roeper Review, 22*, 261–262.

Piirto, J. (1999). *Talented children and adults: Their development and education* (2nd ed.). Upper Saddle River, NJ: Merrill/Prentice Hall.

Rop, C. (1997). Breaking the gender barrier in the physical sciences. *Educational Leadership, 55*(4), 58–60.

Schweigardt, W. J., Worrell, F. C., & Hale, R. J. (2001). Gender differences in the motivation for and selection of courses in a summer program for academically talented students. *Gifted Child Quarterly, 45*, 283–292.

chapter 2

Thinking Creatively About Science

suggestions for primary teachers

by **Karen S. Meador**

t the beginning of life (after their physical needs are satisfied), infants learn through the explorations of their world. They use all of their senses to investigate and enter discovery without any preconceived notions regarding what they will find. Their world is open to chance, and adults improve infants' opportunities for learning by providing appropriate stimulation in a nurturing environment.

Children learn about scientific principles through discovery and investigation, the same way infants learn about their world. This chapter discusses the process skills students need in order to develop basic scientific understanding, emphasizing the need for creative thinking within these endeavors. It also provides examples of differentiated activities that are appropriate for students in kindergarten, first, and second grade.

Creativity and Science

The world needs creative scientists who produce useful, innovative solutions to our problems.

Weisberg (1986) asserted that creative scientists differ from noncreative scientists in at least two distinct ways. First, creative scientists need to be free of rules in order to exercise flexible thinking. This flexibility makes them more likely than others to know when to abandon nonproductive efforts and change approaches to problem solving. Second, creative scientists are also more open to experience, making them more sensitive to problems than their noncreative colleagues. They know when to expend effort on a problem and recognize the potential for significant breakthroughs. They waste little time on simple solutions or on problems for which the solutions would have little impact. The creative scientist may also recognize a problem that others miss, which means they have great potential for producing original research.

Even though our students will not all become scientists, it is important to initiate creative thinking within academic content, maximizing the potential of those who do choose this profession. Additionally, all students who learn to think creatively while engaging in scientific endeavors hone skills applicable to other contents.

Creative Thinking Skills

Adults want students to think flexibly in order to entertain a variety of approaches to solving problems. In science, flexible students think of different types of variables that may impact a phenomenon. Flexible thinkers also have the ability to look at things from multiple perspectives. Flexibility is inherent in remaining open to experiences, which is, as mentioned above, a key difference between creative and noncreative scientists. Youngsters who are open to experiences will be observant during investigations and notice things others may miss.

Resistance to premature closure is an attitude teachers should encourage students to adopt. Teachers do not want students to accept the first explanation or answer that comes to them; rather, they should resist closing on an idea until others have been explored. According to Torrance (1979), when

[f]aced with any incompleteness or unsolved problem, almost everyone tends to jump to some conclusion

immediately. Frequently, this jump is made prematurely—before the person has taken the time to understand the problem, considered important factors involved in the problem, and thought of alternative solutions. (p. 74)

It is necessary to defer judgment in order to resist premature closure and remain open.

Elaboration, another component of creative thinking, enables students to pay careful attention to detail. Teachers want students to be able to provide detailed explanations of their discoveries and plan their own pursuits to answer questions of interest. For further information on components of creative thinking, see *Creative Thinking and Problem Solving for Young Learners* (Meador, 1997).

The Creative Scientific Environment

Primary educators set the stage for discovery and investigation by preparing an environment in which youngsters may encounter appropriate stimulation, igniting their sense of wonder and inviting questions. For example, there may be a container in the classroom in which students and teachers place interesting articles from nature (such as rocks, insects, leaves, and plants). A plastic bucket or box may house interesting gadgets for students to explore and guess their use. In another part of the room, students may find a mechanical object that is being dismantled. For example, the inside of a toaster may prove interesting.

In addition to being physically safe, this environment must also be risk-free for creative thinking and discussion of observed phenomena. Teachers do not want students to squelch their own questions, fearing that others might consider them silly or dumb. At the primary level, questioning and experiential learning lay the basis for later scientific concepts and essential understandings. Charlesworth and Lind (1995) suggested that an added benefit of such experiential learning is that students learn many attitudes and skills that will help them solve authentic problems encountered throughout life.

Science Process Skills

Science process skills are "the most powerful tools we have for producing and arranging information about our world" (Ostlund, 1992, p. v). They are, of course, essential as students learn to think like scientists. Charlesworth and Lind (1995) provided a hierarchy of science process skills and categorized them into basic, intermediate, and advanced levels (see Table 2.1).

Educators may wish to use the hierarchy in the development of typical and differentiated lessons and centers, moving up the process ladder for more able learners. It is vital, however, that students master skills at the basic level since intermediate and advanced process skills depend on mastery of lower level skills. A student cannot successfully infer without first honing key observation techniques. Table 2.2 indicates the correspondence between science process skills and creative thinking.

Examples of Learning Episodes

The following lessons provide opportunities for students to practice basic scientific process skills and creative thinking.

Attribute Socks: Observing

Students practice observation using touch, smell, and sound as they determine the attributes of objects placed inside socks. The socks are tied at the top so students cannot see what's inside. Some students have a difficult time resisting the urge to look inside the socks, so it is important to tie them quite tightly. Dark socks prevent students from seeing the color of the objects if they hold them in the air toward a light.

Objects (such as an empty contact lens container, a softball, a paperweight, and an emery board) are appropriate for attribute socks. Include objects that make a noise such as a sealed box of paper clips or a small baby rattle. Students instinctively want to guess the identity of the object; however, teachers should encourage them to think like a scientist and resist premature closure. Scientists would miss key information if they concluded an experiment the moment the first hypothesis arose. Students

Table 2.1. **Hierarchy of Science Process Skills Categorized by Levels**		
Process Skills Basic Science	**Intermediate Process Skills**	**Advanced Process Skills**
Observing Comparing Classifying Measuring Communicating	Inferring Predicting	Hypothesizing Defining and controlling variables

Note. From *Math and Science for Young Children* (2nd ed., p. 54), by R. Charlesworth & K. K. Lind, 1995, Albany, NY: Delmar. Copyright ©1995 by Delmar Learning. Reprinted with permission of Delmar Learning, a division of Thomson Learning; www.thomsonrights.com; fax (800) 730-2215.

should elaborate and tell about the object by discussing how it feels, its shape, size, weight, and so on. What are its characteristics or attributes?

Attribute Socks Differentiation: Observing, Classifying, and Communicating

A move up the hierarchy of processes to classification provides differentiation for this activity. Students can sort or classify attribute socks into groups based on the characteristics of the objects they contain. A very young child may need to be prodded into sorting by weight or another specific attribute; however, the challenge of the activity arises as students determine their own discriminating factors. Obviously, when students sort into groups based on multiple attributes, (e.g., the four groups of big and hard, big and soft, small and hard, and small and soft), they have added extra complexity to the process. Students practice elaborating and communicating when they articulate the attributes of each of their groups and defend the placement of each attribute sock.

Water on the Move: Predicting, Comparing, and Communicating

Kids like to play in water; yet, this adventure does not have to be messy. Teachers can build upon students' natural

Table 2.2. **Corresponding Skills**

Corresponding Skills	Hierarchy of Science Process Skills	Components of Creative Thinking
Basic Science Process Skills	Observing	Openness to Experience: Being sensitive and observant.
	Comparing	Flexibility: Comparing from multiple angles or viewpoints.
	Classifying	Flexibility and Elaboration: Considering multiple ways in which things might be grouped and providing details about the attributes of categories.
	Measuring	(Creative thinking is not usually required.)
	Communicating	Elaboration: Providing clear and detailed explanations.
Intermediate Process Skills	Inferring	Flexibility: Thinking about various meanings before deciding on the inference.
	Predicting	Flexibility and Creative Convergence*: Considering a variety of different possibilities and then deciding on the most plausible.
Advanced Process Skills	Hypothesizing	Resistance to Premature Closure and Creative Convergence: Making an informed hypothesis after considering multiple possibilities rather than jumping to conclusions.
	Defining and controlling variables	Elaboration: Carefully planning how to control variables.

Note. The author suggests the following definition for creative convergence referenced in the chart above: (1) the act of making a decision or choice regarding a number of options being considered and (2) the process of working with a divergent idea in order to make it plausible, useful, or appropriate.

interest in water to capture their attention for a prediction exercise. Students are open to new experiences when they explore liquid movement on waxed paper. Students use infant eye droppers (found in the pharmaceutical department of discount stores) to place red, yellow, and blue drops of water on waxed paper. These liquids are mixtures of food coloring and water. By gently blowing and dabbing a straw into the liquid, they discover how surface tension affects the shape and movement of the water. It is not, however, necessary to explain the phenomenon to the students. The waxed paper allows the liquid to retain its rounded shape even when students blow the drops across the paper. The shape and movement are analogous to that of liquid mercury. The children also delight in the blending of colors when one colored drop collides with another. This activity could easily be used simply for determining how colors mix to create new ones.

After students have enjoyed the initial water play on waxed paper, they are prepared to predict how the drops will hold their shape and move on foil. These predictions are based on whether the water will react in the same manner on the new surface as it did on the waxed paper. Students must think flexibly as they consider how the new surface may affect the experiment. Communicating by writing their predictions on chart paper prepares them for recording formal hypotheses later in more sophisticated experiments. Students analyze their hypotheses following experimentation on the new surface and then communicate their findings by stating how their results confirm or disprove the prediction. They compare similarities and differences in the water shape and movement on the waxed paper and the foil. The form of communication—from a simple tape recording of the students' comments, to a more formal writing of the prediction and the results—depends upon the students' age and ability. Similarly, their age, ability, and interests help determine the advisability of continuing this format with other surfaces. Experimentation with cooking paper, freezer paper, glass, and construction paper also provide interesting opportunities for prediction and discovery.

Water on the Move Differentiation: Defining and Controlling Variables

Rather than continuing the above activity with multiple surfaces, educators may differentiate it by varying the liquid used in the experiment and asking students to make predictions regarding the type of liquid, rather than type of surface. This calls for even greater flexibility in thinking. Dishwashing liquid and cooking oil are good choices for alternate liquids.

Mixing dishwashing liquid with water (gently to prevent suds) provides students with useful information as they discover that the surface tension of the water lowers since the dishwashing liquid is a surfactant. Manufacturers of detergent use this surface-active agent to improve saturation. Adults can add dishwashing agents to other liquids, such as weed killer, to facilitate efforts to saturate the leaves of unwanted vegetation.

Differentiation

Some educators may feel that, when gifted children encounter opportunities for free exploration and discovery, they differentiate their own learning. It is certainly true that their curiosity can manifest in the form of questions, and the answers to these questions facilitate deeper understanding. Yet, this is not enough.

Student questions should guide teachers to plan differentiated lessons and exploratory activities; however, planned differentiation should also be based on the educator's clear understanding of how to add depth and complexity to the core curriculum. Teachers must not leave differentiation to chance and expect that the gifted child will always find challenge. Rather, it is important to hold clear expectations for the differentiated learning. Unplanned differentiation can be compared to going to the grocery store without a list: The refrigerator and pantry may be filled afterward, but the food purchased may not be what is needed to prepare the planned recipe.

Teachers should plan for gifted students to exercise more advanced science process skills. As previously mentioned in the attribute socks activity, while typical students observe, high-ability students classify and communicate. Teachers may likewise consider planning for gifted students to utilize more advanced levels of thinking in Bloom's taxonomy (Bloom, Engelhart, Furst, Hill, & Krathwohl, 1956). For example, while young children gain knowledge regarding the effect of mixing baking soda and vinegar, students with high abilities in science may quickly jump into analyzing the difference between this mixture and other white compounds mixed with vinegar. The latter may be followed by a synthesis of information about mixtures and an examination of recipes to hypothesize why certain ingredients are used.

Differentiation also results when teachers plan for students to use combined, rather than isolated, creative thinking skills. Students exercise fluent and flexible thinking when they generate multiple suggestions as to why the incline of a ramp affects the distance a toy travels after going down it. Students may create a chart explaining the relationship between incline and distance traveled, and in the process they are combining fluency, flexibility, originality, and elaboration.

Teachers can also plan for gifted students to encounter more perplexing phenomena during explorations. For example, some young students are ready to see that size does not necessarily indicate weight, a phenomenon they can explore by using a balance scale to compare objects in which weight and size do or do not correspond. Differentiation for students with high abilities in the sciences may occur as they weigh objects that contradict their original assumptions regarding size and weight relationships—a large object weighs less than a small one (e.g., a small rock may weigh more than a larger softball).

Conclusion

Unfortunately, just as a deprived infant may not develop appropriately, the young student denied opportunities for science investigation may not form the needed foundation for future scientific understandings. Even older students who make outstanding grades in science due to their ability to memorize and retain information may lack the depth of understanding necessary to make contributions to the field. Many students who enjoy experimentation do not exercise creative thinking during their investigations.

Teachers need to facilitate learning experiences through which students have sufficient opportunities to develop true scientific understanding, science process skills, and corresponding creative thinking skills. As primary teachers provide ample opportunities for experimentation and discovery at a young age, they encourage scientific genius and enable problem solvers.

References

Bloom, B. S., Engelhart, M. D., Furst, E. J., Hill, W. H., & Krathwohl, D. R. (1956). *Taxonomy of educational objectives. Handbook I: Cognitive domain.* New York: Longmans Green.

Charlesworth, R., & Lind, K. K. (1995). *Math and science for young children* (2nd ed.). Albany, NY: Delmar.

Meador, K. S. (1997). *Creative thinking and problem solving for young learners.* Englewood, CO: Teacher Ideas Press.

Ostlund, K. L. (1992). *Science process skills: Assessing hands-on student performance.* New York: Addison-Wesley.

Torrance, E. P. (1979). *The search for satori & creativity.* Buffalo, NY: Creative Education Foundation.

Weisberg, R. W. (1986). *Creativity: Genius and other myths.* New York: Freeman.

section two

Acceleration and Enrichment in Science

chapter 3

Developing an Early Passion for Science Through Competitions

by **Frances A. Karnes** *and* **Tracy L. Riley**

*t*he most recent Trends in International Mathematics and Science Study (TIMSS; National Center for Education Statistics, 2004) showed that, in 2003, U.S. fourth graders were outperformed in mathematics by 11 countries and in science by 5. The TIMSS results also found no measurable changes in the average mathematics and science scores of U.S. fourth graders between 1995 and 2003. Even more alarmingly, the available data suggest that the performance of U.S. fourth graders in both mathematics and science was lower in 2003 than in 1995 relative to the 14 other countries that also participated in both studies. While U.S. eighth graders improved their math and science scores between 1995 and 2003, they were still outscored by 14 countries in mathematics and 8 countries in science.

Two major problems that are frequently cited for the U.S.'s poor performance are that (a) science and math teachers teach out of their fields and (b) few high school seniors take advanced classes, especially Advanced Placement courses.

While these and other reasons for the poor performance will not be rectified in a short period of time, students may become more productively involved in various fields of science through competitions. An early introduction to such activities may foster and nurture a passion for science and serve as one of the many ways to boost further participation in advanced science classes and bolster our rank among the top nations in performance.

Those students who classify as top performers in science bring to the classroom a unique set of characteristics, thus setting them apart from their peers (George, 1997). Scientifically gifted students make close observations of the things around them. They are problem seekers, as well as solution finders. Experimenting with ideas while enjoying the pleasure of not knowing the answer often absorbs their minds over long periods of time. They are passionate about science, as indicated by their motivation, persistence, inventiveness, and natural curiosity.

While these broad generalizations can be clearly seen in many gifted students, it is essential for teachers to recognize and cater to unique, individual needs. Cropper (1998) identified competitions as one tool for gaining "insight into the gifted student's scholastic and creative functioning" (p. 30) so that teachers can begin planning and programming for those needs. By placing scientifically gifted students in an atmosphere of challenges via competitions, the spotlight shines on their abilities.

Aside from being used as a means of identifying individual needs, competitions can also be used to spark motivation (Cropper, 1998). Being motivated to experiment, thus thinking and acting like a scientist, can lead to a lifelong love of science. Brandwein (1995) stated that motivation is part of a predisposing factor that leads to the development of scientific talent. Aside from motivation, he identified two other factors: persistence and questioning.

Naturally, competitions can also serve as part of the activating factor necessary for developing scientific will and skill (Brandwein, 1995). The activation for student development of talent is often found in the school climate and environment that serve to facilitate learning. By recognizing and rewarding scientific talent, as well as facilitating development, schools send boys and girls a strong message about what is valued in students. A strong sense of pride flourishes for both the school and community as students' abilities are acknowledged (Williams, 1986).

Finally, competitions tap the underlying principles for teaching science to gifted students. They provide students with opportunities for studying both the content and processes of science while also debating real problems and issues. Furthermore, competitions provide a platform for launching in-depth studies on a wide variety of topics. They also give a shift in roles for the teacher as he or she coaches and facilitates learning, as opposed to teaching in the more traditional sense. Competition can serve as a unique catalyst for growth and development of scientific talent while maintaining the tried and true guidelines of appropriate instruction for gifted students.

The competitions available are many (Karnes & Riley, 2005). They vary in design, purpose, and audience, thus affording students a smorgasbord of opportunities. Selecting competitions that best match perceived student strengths and interests ensures positive outcomes for participants. Student choice is also important, as supported by Cropper (1998), who encouraged a "meaningful degree of student participation in the competitive assessment process" (p. 30).

The amount of time spent on preparation and participation in competitions also varies. Careful calendar planning in advance of the school year for "peak" times is one technique teachers use to ensure that day-to-day classroom routines are not consumed by competitions. Teachers also need to take into account the following four variables when scheduling:

1. *Type of project or product.* These vary in depth and breadth, from essays, to posters, to long-term experiments.
2. *Home and school.* Students can work on competitions in either environment, though a balance may be most desirable.
3. *Curricular fit.* Objectives that are well met through competitions may justify more classroom time.
4. *Individual pace and style.* Whether in groups or going solo, students will need varying amounts of time in order to complete entries satisfactorily.

Though teachers need to take a realistic view of the amount of time competitions might take, part of it also requires teachers to recognize the many factors that play into time management. Selection, student choice, and preparation for participation in competitions, coupled with the variety of scientific learning opportunities, open up a world of excitement for the classroom.

Science Competitions

The following examples are but a smattering of the many possibilities available for nurturing the passion in scientifically gifted students.

Federal Junior Duck Stamps Conservation and Design Program

Science combined with art is a great way to enhance learning. To learn wetlands awareness through the arts, the Federal Junior Duck Stamps Program was established in 1989. It is open to all students in kindergarten through grade 12. Local schools are mailed information during October. A free curriculum and video are available upon the request of a teacher. The competition is specific to the design of a Junior Duck Stamp involving North American ducks, swans, or geese in natural habitats. Judges are selected within each state for that level of judging, with the criteria being the accurate depiction of wildlife in its natural habitat. Awards include a certificate of participation for each student who enters a design, 199 ribbons across all age categories, and a State Best of Show ribbon. The national first-place winner receives a $5,000 award and a trip to Washington, DC, to attend the adult Federal Duck Stamp Contest. For more information, visit http://duckstamps.fws.gov/junior/junior.htm.

A Pledge and a Promise Environmental Awards

Another competition focusing on the area of environmental science is the A Pledge and a Promise Environmental Awards. Developed to recognize the outstanding efforts of school groups in the areas of environmental awareness and action, the awards are service-oriented with academics included. The focus is primarily on the actions that school groups take to help protect the natural resources of our planet. All ages may apply for these awards within four categories: K–5, 6–8, 9–12, and college. These groups apply by submitting completed environmental projects or works-in-progress to better the planet around them. Creativity, innovation, measurable effects, and benefits to the community and the environment are some of the criteria used to judge the projects. Another criterion is the transferable quality of the project: Do they serve as a model for others? Do the projects offer a long-term gain for the environment and community?

Projects must be student-driven. The judges are selected from national environmental groups. The awards for each age group are: first place—$12,500; second place—$5,000; third place—$2,500. The grand prize of $20,000 is awarded to the one project that is judged the best overall in any category. Great advice for those wishing to participate is to complete the application accurately and to be sure that the project is creative and student-driven. Write for information to A Pledge and a Promise Environmental Awards, Education Department, Sea World, 7007 Sea World Dr., Orlando, FL 32821.

President's Environmental Youth Awards

The President's Environmental Youth Awards offer students of all age groups an opportunity to become an environmental force within the community. Students may compete as individuals, school classes, schools, public interest groups, summer camps, and youth organizations. They are recognized for their efforts to make and keep the world around us a safer, cleaner place to live. The judging panel considers the following: environmental need for the project; environmental appropriateness; accomplishment of goals and long-term environmental benefits derived; evidence of the young person's initiative; and clarity and effectiveness of presentation. A certificate signed by the President of the United States is given to all regional winners. The national winners with one project sponsor receive an all-expense-paid trip to Washington, DC, where they participate in the annual National Awards Ceremony and cash prizes are given. For additional information, visit http://www.epa.gov/enviroed/awards.html.

National Science Olympiad

The purpose of the National Science Olympiad is to improve science skills and knowledge in the areas of life science, general science, earth science, chemistry, physics, and biology. Medals and certificates are awarded to students in grades 2–12 who participate. For more information, visit http://www.soinc.org.

NASA Student Involvement Program

Students are usually fascinated by the study of space and can apply their knowledge in the NASA Student Involvement Program. The competition was established to encourage students in grades K–12 to become involved in the hands-on educational experience of space science. There are several national competitions appropriate for the elementary and junior high school levels. K–1 and 2–4 students can compete in "My Planet, Earth" and "Science & Technology Journalism," while students in grades 5–8 can compete in "Science & Technology Journalism," "Aerospace Technology Engineering Challenge," "Design a Lunar-Based Mission to Mars," and "Watching Earth Change." Students and teachers can win trips to NASA centers, internships with NASA scientists, space camp scholarships, medals, ribbons, certificates, and national recognition. For more information, visit http://www.nsip.net/about/index.cfm.

Conclusion

In maximizing the potential of competitions by encouraging and facilitating student participation, teachers can begin the journey toward the development of passion for science, even in the earliest primary years. If poor science performance is to be overcome and gifted students are to take their place among the best and brightest on the planet, that passion must be developed and nurtured. The earlier this appetite for science is developed and enhanced, the sooner we will begin to see change occur. In order to bolster our ranks in the international marketplace of science education, we must begin with the enhancement of science for gifted children.

References

Brandwein, P. F. (1995). *Science talent in the young expressed within ecologies of achievement* (RBDM 9510). Storrs: National Research on the Gifted and Talented, University of Connecticut.

Cropper, C. (1998). Is competition an effective classroom tool for the gifted student? *Gifted Child Today, 21*(3), 28–30.

George, D. (1997). Making a place for the bright sparks: The challenge of the gifted child in science. *Science Education Newsletter, 133,* 1–2.

Karnes, F. A., & Riley, T. L. (2005). *Competitions: Maximizing your abilities* (Rev. ed.). Waco, TX: Prufrock Press.

National Center for Education Statistics. (2004). *TIMSS 2003 results.* Retrieved January 4, 2005, from http://nces.ed.gov/timss/Results03.asp

Williams, A. T. (1986). Academic game bowls as a teaching/learning tool. *Gifted Child Today, 9*(1), 2–5.

chapter 4

Developing the Talents of Teacher/Scientists

by **George Robinson**

ne of the best things teachers can do to develop the talents of young scientists is to do science themselves. Teachers need to practice doing practical science research, with the emphasis on doing if they are to impart the joy of science to their students. Linguists tell us that the best way to learn a language is through immersion. Go to a foreign country, live there, and speak the language daily. Likewise, if teachers want to become better scientists or researchers, they need to go on an expedition and immerse themselves in the day-to-day language of science and research. By conducting this type of personal investigation, teachers can travel to locations worldwide, learn new skills, make new friends, contribute to the growing knowledge about planet Earth, and bring back valuable insights about teaching science to their classrooms. Teachers inevitably receive more respect from their students because they not only "talk the talk" about science, but because they have also "walked the walk" as practicing professionals in the field. There are many opportunities now available through the Internet for teachers to be part of a research team in the field.

Part I: Field Research Opportunities

National Oceanographic and Atmospheric Administration (NOAA) Teacher at Sea Program
http://www.tas.noaa.gov/

The National Oceanographic and Atmospheric Administration (NOAA) administers the Teacher at Sea Program. Research vessels are available to accommodate teachers who wish to assist oceanographers and marine biologists in research on such topics as ocean floor mapping and shark behavior. One no-frills expedition offered by NOAA is a 3-day trip from Miami to Mississippi towing a plankton net. Teacher/scientists aboard this ship work 8-hour shifts pulling up the tow and examining what they find. The expedition is not about books or coursework, just getting your hands wet and learning firsthand about what's in the ocean.

Research at SEA
http://www.sea.edu/sea2000/admission2000/Teachers.htm

SEA Seamester's 6-week program is an oceanographic research experience for middle and high school teachers. It gives them the opportunity to explore the oceanic environment while learning about the scientific research process firsthand. The program uses a sailing research vessel as the platform and utilizes the expertise of oceanographers from the Woods Hole scientific community. Participants in Research at SEA learn how research scientists pose and attempt to answer scientific questions. The goal is to enhance the teacher's ability to bring investigative learning into their classrooms.

Earth Watch Institute
http://www.earthwatch.org

Earthwatch is another organization that seeks out volunteers to participate in research trips, from the ruins of ancient Pompeii, to the zebras of Kenya. Participants support research scientists in their field work collecting data. So far, 3,500 volunteers have worked with 120 research scientists in more than 50 countries all around the world.

The JASON Project
http://www.jasonproject.org

Another excellent program that solicits both teacher and student volunteers is the JASON Project. Dr. Ballard, famous for discovering the *Titanic*, has for the last 12 years been going around the world on expeditions that are broadcast live back to school audiences. Regular students and teachers who have an interest in doing science on a remote site help with the nuts-and-bolts work of assisting field biologists, oceanographers, and technicians on these expeditions.

The Amazon/Andes Rainforest Workshop
http://www.birds.cornell.edu/cfw/classroom/amazon_workshop.html

The Amazon/Andes Rainforest Workshop allows participants to become involved with field research that is currently underway in the area. Participants explore a variety of topics such as rainforest ecology, rainforest conservation, tropical mammals, neotropical insects, tropical birds, and medicinal use of plants. The National Science Teachers Association and the National Biology Teachers Association cosponsor the workshop.

University of California at Berkeley's Research Expeditions Program
http://www.berkeley.edu

University of California Research Expeditions Program (UREP)
http://www.extension.ucdavis.edu/urep

University of California, Irvine, Center for International Education
http://www.cie.uci.edu/iop

The University of California Research Expeditions Program

combines a University of California research team with volunteers to undertake research in variety of areas, including archaeology, animal studies, geology, arts and culture, and environmental conservation. Current research expeditions include prehistoric settlers of Lake Titicaca in Peru and saving Orinoco Geese in Venezuela, gray whales of the Pacific Northwest in British Columbia, and ancient reefs of the Outback in Australia. The program at Irvine offers teachers the opportunities for internships, volunteer positions, field research, and teaching overseas.

Conservation Education Diving Awareness Marine Research (CEDAM)
http://www.cedam.org

A special mention must be given to CEDAM, which stands for their interests in Conservation, Education, Diving, Awareness, and Marine Research, headed by underwater naturalists Rick and Susan Sammon. This organization assists marine science and research projects by paring marine scientists who need assistance with their research in marine biology and marine/terrestrial archeology with volunteer divers who want to participate in scientific research. Current expeditions include textiles of West Africa, an archaeological site in Italy, an excavation in Bolivia, an archaeological trip to Ecuador, and exploring human origins in Tanzania.

Bermuda Biological Station for Research., Inc.
http://www.bbsr.edu

Located in the mid-Atlantic, this station for research in biology and zoology offers courses, workshops, a library, and dive facilities. The focus is on oceanography and coral reefs.

The Center for Integrating Research and Learning
http://ret.magnet.fsu.edu

The Center for Integrating Research and Learning at the National High Magnetic Field Laboratory offers a program entitled "Research Experiences for Teachers." Funded by the National Science Foundation, the 6-week residential program provides K–12 teachers with the opportunity to participate in real-world science research.

EcoTeach
http://www.ecoteach.com

This ecotourism company provides sea turtle research tours in Costa Rica for teachers and their students (with 20 students, teachers go free) or teacher-only study tours with university credit.

International Field Studies
http://www.intlfieldstudies.com

International Field Studies (IFS) is a public, nonprofit, educational organization that promotes and assists teachers with field study programs. IFS functions as a facilitator for educational groups seeking expertise and logistical support. IFS staff members, experienced field instructors, and resource materials are available to assist teachers and group leaders with educational development, site planning, and budgeting for a successful, comprehensive field program. By working with IFS to develop a proposed field study, teachers are able to offer their students high-quality field study opportunities that would not be feasible without such a collective effort.

WhaleNet Teacher Opportunities and Classes
http://whale.wheelock.edu/whalenet-stuff/prof_dev.html

WhaleNet offers teachers professional development field courses in Massachusetts, Quebec, and Bermuda and provides links to many other opportunities across the country.

Introduction to Coastal Marine Ecology of the Florida Keys
http://www.mrdf.org/marinelab_teacher.htm

MarineLab in Key Largo, FL, offers a 1-week intensive field program of subtropical/tropical marine ecology geared toward middle and secondary school science teachers.

NASA's Summer High School Apprenticeship
Research Program (SHARP)
http://www.mtsibase.com/sharp

Sponsored by the National Aeronautics and Space Administration (NASA) since its inception in 1980, the Summer High School Apprenticeship Research Program (SHARP) is designed for students who have demonstrated a strong interest in and aptitude for mathematics, science, engineering, and technology. Each year, approximately 400 students are selected to participate in SHARP for a minimum of 8 weeks during the summer. Some of NASA's top science professionals mentor qualified students while conducting cutting-edge research and working on state-of-the-art equipment.

Part II: Backyard Research

Traveling to exotic locations to do field research is definitely an experience that a teacher will remember and relate to his or her class with enthusiasm. For those who are unable to travel far from home, there are other opportunities to undertake scientific research closer to home.

Cornell Lab of Ornithology
http://birds.cornell.edu

Researchers at the Cornell Lab of Ornithology are enlisting citizen-scientists to help collect data for researchers' studies of bird populations. This collection can be done in a person's backyard or in a teacher's schoolyard through programs such as eBird, Project PigeonWatch, Birds in Forested Landscapes, and Project FeederWatch. Ornithologists use this information to learn what birds are found where and how bird populations might be changing over time. For example, scientists at the lab are tracking the spread of house finch eye disease. This disease causes conjunctivitis in birds, and many die because their poor vision prevents them from finding food and avoiding predators. Thanks to the efforts of citizen-scientists, researchers have been able to track the spread of disease through a wild population of animals for the first time.

National Wildlife Federation's Backyard Wildlife Habitat
http://www.nwf.org/backyardwildlifehabitat

The National Wildlife Federation's Backyard Wildlife Habitat program involves volunteers in creating a certified habitat in their own backyard or in their schoolyard. Citizen-naturalists participate in formal data collecting and monitoring projects to help songbirds, butterflies, and other wildlife.

International Migratory Bird Day (IMBD)
http://www.americanbirding.org/imbd

International Migratory Bird Day celebrates the return of millions of migratory birds to their breeding areas. Individuals, groups, and schools participate in IMBD by organizing birding tours, conducting surveys, and holding festivals and workshops with the purpose of educating and encouraging others in their community to join in the conservation of migratory birds and their habitats.

National Audubon Society Christmas Bird Count
http://www.audubon.org/bird/cbc

The Audubon Society sponsors an annual hemispheric early-winter bird census during which volunteers count individual bird and bird species. Data provide valuable insights into the long-term health of bird populations and the environment.

4th of July Butterfly Count
http://www.naba.org/counts.html

This ongoing program collects census data on the butterflies of North America and publishes the results. Volunteer participants select a count area and conduct a 1-day census of butterflies sighted. Counts are usually held sometime around July 4.

Monarch Watch
http://www.monarchwatch.org

This outreach program promotes the conservation of monarch butterflies and involves thousands of students and adults in a cooperative tagging study of the monarch's fall migration.

Keeping Track
http://www.keepingtrackinc.org

Keeping Track is a research/education project through which volunteers are trained in wildlife track and sign identification either in Vermont or at a local site in a participant's home state. Cumulative data are used to aid local and regional planners in making informed decisions about wildlife habitat protection.

North American Amphibian Monitoring Program (NAAMP)
http://www.pwrc.usgs.gov/naamp

This is a project through which volunteers monitor amphibian populations. Projects include frog call surveys and terrestrial salamander monitoring.

Save Our Streams
http://www.iwla.org/sos

This is a grassroots river conservation program through which volunteers are trained to monitor and restore local waterways. Projects exist in all 50 states. They have an excellent online macroinvertebrate identification program.

Part III: Virtual Expeditions

For people who like to travel in cyberspace, there are expeditions that do not require them to leave the comforts of their living rooms. Online adventures to worldwide locations, as well as to outer space destinations, are possible for both the classroom teacher and his or her students. The following are a few of the many journeys possible.

The Biology Project: The University of Arizona
http://www.biology.arizona.edu

This "Web lab" simulates the potential spread of HIV through a population. Each participant exchanges virtual body fluids with other participants, some of whom are HIV+, and a computer-simulated ELISA (a basic test for the presence of HIV) illustrates the spread of the disease. In addition to the HIV simulation, there is another simulation that is intriguing: DNA Profiling. In this simulation, students learn the concepts and techniques behind DNA profiling used in forensic and paternity labs. They solve DNA paternity tests and missing people's problems.

Education Program @ Earthwatch Institute
http://www.earthwatch.org/education/us.html

This program enables teachers and students to collaborate with scientists doing field research at locations worldwide. Teachers and students who choose not to join researchers in person through the Earthwatch volunteer program can now learn from a distance.

The JASON Project
http://www.marinelab.sarasota.fl.us/~kristen/jason.phtml

The JASON Projects offers a yearlong multimedia interdisciplinary program for students and teachers in grades 5–8. The program integrates video programming, satellite transmissions, classroom instruction, and online activities so that students and teachers may learn through hands-on inquiry.

Journey North
http://www.learner.org/jnorth

Journey North is an Internet-based learning adventure that engages students in a global study of wildlife migration and seasonal change. Students are linked with scientists who provide their expertise directly to the classroom.

Moonlink
http://www.space-explorers.com

Moonlink is the first Internet-based program that directly involves students in a live space mission. Students participate in an interactive simulation of the Lunar Prospector Mission and actual data analysis for an 8,700-square-mile section of the moon.

Virtual Pig Dissection
http://www.whitman.edu/biology/vpd/main.html

Students dissect a virtual pig and along the way learn about anatomical references, sexing their pig, the digestive system, the excretory system, the circulatory system, the reproductive system, the respiratory system, and the nervous system.

NASA Ames Research Center Volunteer Opportunities
http://quest.arc.nasa.gov

Located in Mountain View, this interactive education facility uses webcasts and chat rooms to teach kids what happens behind the closed doors of NASA.

SitesALIVE!
http://sitesalive.com

SitesALIVE! is an interactive, multidisciplinary education Web site that connects students in the classroom to adventures, expeditions, and events around the world as they are unfolding.

Part IV: A Teacher's Tale

Steve Pesick, the science department coordinator for Mt. Pleasant Central Schools in Thornwood, NY, not only offers a top-notch authentic science program in his high school, but has adapted the program to the needs of middle school students. Pesick finds he can empathize with students who are undertaking rigorous scientific investigations under the tutelage of a mentor because he was recently awarded the Lloyd Bridges Expedition Scholarship by CEDAM International.

He was paired with Kathleen Sullivan, a researcher in marine biology from the University of Miami, to assist her with her research on groupers in the Caribbean. Steve's tour of duty consisted of spending 1 week aboard the Turks and Cacaos Aggressor with 10 other volunteers. Their research responsibilities were divided between diving in the ocean and working on the deck. Their main job was to bring up groupers to the deck. In order to do this, they had to lower and service the fish traps, bait them with cat food and injured conch, inflate the airbags to raise the cage when a grouper was trapped, and then transfer the grouper on to the deck. Once the fish was on the deck, the second team took over anesthetizing the grouper and then weighing, measuring, and tagging it. Then, they would snip a fin clip for later DNA analysis and dunk the grouper in fresh water to collect isopods to find out what creatures lived on it. Finally, they would return the grouper to the sea. The dive team then escorted the grouper back down to 50 feet and observed the released fish as it readjusted to life under the sea.

In addition to collecting groupers, the dive team also had the responsibility of conducting an abundance and diversity grouper survey of the collecting area. This was accomplished by having three teams of two divers follow three different 50-meter transects and record what was seen in the areas.

The Rewards

Participating in a scientific expedition offers many rewards for the science teacher. The top benefit is the renewed enthusiasm the teacher has for his or her subject. According to Mr. Pesick,

> This enthusiasm, this feeling of rejuvenation will definitely rub off on my students. This enthusiasm comes from the sense that you are doing something that no one else has done before. Unlike some of the science questions in the textbook that are prescribed, presented, and previously solved, no one in the world can tell you what these results will be. Teachers can get their

students excited about science by involving them in real-world problems and issues.

In addition, to a renewed vigor for science, Mr. Pesick also brought back to his classroom a sense of what is important for his students to know about doing science: accuracy and precision, the need for practice, and the need for hands-on involvement. He said,

> Dr. Sullivan constantly stressed that we couldn't give a measurement of "about 36 or 37 centimeters." It had to be exactly 36.4 centimeters. Since groupers grow at the rate of one centimeter a year, this information is necessary for a precise and valid understanding of the fish population.

In order for students to become precise in their measurement or recording of observations, a lot of practice is needed. Before Mr. Pesick and his team went into the water to survey the grouper population, Dr. Sullivan had them practice walking along a transect on deck to catalogue the size and type of groupers that were pictured along the route. A certain standard of accuracy was required before the teams were allowed to dive. Not meeting the standard meant doing it again until they did. Mr. Pesick is now using this concept with his sixth-grade authentic research science class, which is studying birds in the Cornell Lab of Ornithology's Bird Watch Program. Before conducting the bird watch survey for 30 minutes a day for 15 days at their homes, students learn to identify the birds through slides. Mr. Pesick then takes them outside once a week for field practice in identifying the birds at the various bird feeders around the campus. This practice assures a more precise and accurate accounting for the bird survey, which means the surveys will be more valid and reliable.

Measuring and weighing the groupers, dunking them in a fresh water bath to recover isopods, and then tagging them are activities that brought personal involvement and meaning to this research project for Mr. Pesick. To give his students a similar hands-on experience, he had them go out on to the school grounds and collect bugs and insects to learn about classification. With careful, focused inspection, his students were able to categorize bugs as creatures that drink their food because of their pointed mouth and insects as creatures that chew their food because of their mandibles.

Because of Mr. Pesick's experience as a researcher, he has initiated programs in his science classes that highlight the student as researcher: a research expedition to the coral reefs of Key Largo; and Cornell Lab of Ornithology's FeederWatch Program.

Research Expedition to Key Largo

October 2000 marked the fifth expedition Mr. Pesick sponsored for his students to conduct research on the abundance and diversity of fish on the coral reefs off Key Largo. The overall research question, design, analysis of results, and reporting of results is the responsibility of the Reef Environmental Education Foundation (REEF). His student scuba divers and snorkelers help gather the data needed by REEF. His students follow the protocols established by the organization for identifying and quantifying the different fish on the reef. Data is encoded on a reporting sheet and sent to REEF for inclusion in their worldwide data bank for use by professionals in the field. Students benefit from the REEF encounter by honing their observational skills, learning how to record data accurately, and presenting what they experienced at their annual symposium.

An average of 20 students and parents participate each year. The Saw Mill River Audubon Society has provided grants to several of the students each year to help offset the cost of the trip. Students stay in Key Largo for 5 days. During this time, they receive instruction about the Coral Reef Habitat from Florida Keys National Marine Sanctuary personnel, fish identification classes from the REEF Foundation, a dive to the Jules Verne Underwater Habitat sponsored by the National Oceanic and Atmospheric Administration, as well as water quality monitoring experiences in the bay.

Project FeederWatch

This program introduces students to bird identification, bird behavior, bird habitats, and the protocol used to record observations in the field. For example, one of Mr. Pesick's students had developed this question: "How do birds react to human-made sounds as opposed to natural sounds?" To research this question, she set up a platform feeder outside the science classroom. She attached a speaker to the feeder. A tape-recorder was placed inside the classroom and connected to the speaker. Each morning at 7:00 a.m. for 3 weeks, she played a different tape of such natural sounds as moose calls and canary songs, and then human-made sounds such as the human voice and classical music. She confirmed her hypothesis that birds would not be frightened away by the natural sounds, but would fly away at the human-made sounds. She submitted her results to Cornell Lab of Ornithology's publication *Classroom Birdscope*.

Conclusion

Whether a teacher like Mr. Pesick undertakes science research in an exotic locale, in his or her own backyard, or virtually in cyberspace, the results are beneficial for the students. The teacher's enthusiasm for doing research is extended to the students, who also share in the joy of doing science. The teacher's expertise is likewise shared with students through insights and procedures that make the path of a novice researcher easier to walk. The old adage that success breeds success is certainly true here. Mr. Pesick has just been selected as a JASON Argonaut and will be assisting Dr. Robert Ballard off the coast of California with teacher and student research on marine and terrestrial ecosystems of the Channel Islands.

chapter 5

Working With Gifted Science Students in a Public High School Environment

one school's approach

by **Mephie Ngoi** *and* **Mark Vondracek**

he Chemistry/Physics Program at Evanston Township High School was designed in 1952 to provide the most advanced and motivated science students with a challenging college-preparatory science experience. This is a demanding and rigorous study of physical science and mathematics that extends over a 3-year period, beginning in 10th grade. During this year, students take a full year of combined high school honors chemistry and physics at an accelerated pace. In grades 11 and 12, students take college-level chemistry and calculus-based physics during alternating semesters. Until recently, most students in this program would also take calculus (advanced placement Calculus BC) and advanced multivariable calculus during this time. In general, students selected to participate in this program are bright and highly motivated. They are usually ranked in the upper 5% of the student body (school population 3,100).

Each year, however, there is a smaller subset of these students who tend to have exceptional talents in mathematics and science that noticeably exceed those of the typical student in our Chemistry/Physics Program. They tend to master mathematics and science concepts quickly. They are inquisitive, and they tend to display a scientific insight that is far superior to that of most individuals. We classify students in this group as gifted in science and mathematics, while the bulk of the students in our program can be classified as accelerated students.

Just what are the criteria used in identifying a student as gifted? Some educators may label a student who gets top scores on a science assessment tool as being gifted in science. Others may consider a student who consistently maintains a perfect score in a yearlong course as gifted. We present other criteria that we have used to identify gifted students in our Chemistry/Physics Program. We also discuss the different approaches that we have used to keep these students highly challenged and motivated.

Concept Attainment and Gifted Students

The approach we have taken in building the curriculum for our Chemistry/Physics Program has been the emphasis on the attainment of key scientific concepts. Because of the interdisciplinary nature of the program, it was decided to identify key concepts that are necessary to the mastery of chemistry and physics. Examples of concepts that were identified in this category include the concepts of an atom, of force, of energy, and of rate, just to name a few. The importance of these concepts in understanding chemistry and physics is undeniable. One can not discuss Newton's laws of motion without introducing the concept of rate. Likewise, the study of rate of chemical reactions is a major area of study for all aspiring chemists. The concept of force is equally fundamental to the understanding of physics and chemistry. One needs to understand the concept of force in order to understand the concept of bond length in chemistry. The study of intermolecular forces of attraction between molecules is another example that illustrates the importance of this concept in mastering chemistry. These and other concepts are introduced to the students throughout the 3-year sequence of the Chemistry/Physics Program.

Many scientists and science educators have always recognized the need to build scientific knowledge around conceptual schemes. Jackman proposed as far back as 1904 an elementary science curriculum that emphasized the understanding of scientific concepts. Conant (1947), in his writings and reports, also recommended the use of concepts as the major building blocks for the structure of science curricula. Concepts are very important in all areas of science for several reasons. They can be used as legitimate means for organizing scientific facts into meaningful entities. This is the approach that was taken in the Science Department at Evanston Township High School when a physics course known as Conceptual Physics was created for students weak in mathematics. In this course, students are exposed to major physics concepts without requiring rigorous mathematical treatment. These concepts can also be used to integrate scientific knowledge across the various areas of science and facilitate the transfer of learning to new situations.

Indeed, many studies have shown that transfer of learning is greatly facilitated by organizing learning experiences around concepts. Kuslan and Stone (1968) stated to this effect: "Learning which is conceptually oriented is much less likely to be forgotten than learning of isolated facts and principles" (p. 80). The same argument was also espoused by Allport (1937) when he stated that "only when a general principle is understood as applicable to two or more fields does the training in one carry over to the others" (p. 277).

If concepts do facilitate transfer of learning, it is more likely that concept attainment or formation occurs when a student begins to generalize from specific instances of a concept to a class of such instances. This generalization process requires transfer of learning from a specific to a whole class of instances of a given concept. Students who can transfer learning of a given concept are generally referred to as having great insight. For instance, in physics, it is one thing to be able to learn details about a specific force like gravity, but most students are not able to take the next intellectual step and make a connection between gravity and all other forces. This step would include understanding both similarities and differences between gravity and other individual types of forces at both the conceptual and mathematical levels. A gifted student on his or her own may be able to identify a deeper connection between gravity and electromagnetic forces through the fundamental concept of flux and fields or perhaps understand the difference between gravity and the strong nuclear force when introduced to a concept called "asymtotic freedom." These identifications are made through highly abstract mathematical reasoning, and typical Advanced Placement students (i.e., accelerated students) are not able to think at this level.

We have used this ability to transfer learning from specific instances of a concept to a whole class of such instances as a means of distinguishing between gifted and accelerated students. In fact, gifted students display superior scientific insight compared to accelerated students because of their concept attainment, which allows them to transfer learning from specific instances of a concept to a whole class of such instances. We have also used the ability to apply attained concepts to solve problems at high levels of cognition as evidence of being gifted. Such an ability requires mastery of both concrete and abstract reasoning.

Because of their mastery of abstract reasoning, gifted students in the physical sciences also tend to excel in the area of mathematics. The students whom we have identified as gifted in science can identify instances of concepts that were previously learned with great ease in our Chemistry/Physics Program. The gifted students tend to have taken AP Calculus BC at least by grade 7 and some even by grade 9 or 10. In grade 12, they usually take Multivariable Calculus. Some even take higher level mathematics as independent studies. Still others go to Northwestern University to take more advanced mathematics classes.

Accelerated students, on the other hand, are those with an above-average intellectual ability who usually attain concepts by a combination of talent, acquisition of skills through repetitive drills, and hard work. They usually have a mastery of concrete reasoning, plus a fair amount of abstract reasoning. They are typically not as advanced mathematically as those whom we have labeled as gifted. They tend to take AP Calculus AB or BC by grade 12. It should be noted that AB Calculus is a full-year AP course that covers materials that are typically presented during the first semester of BC Calculus. On the other hand, BC

Calculus is a full-year AP course that is taught at a faster pace and covers materials generally taught in the first-year two-semester college calculus course.

One may wonder just what evaluation process we use in distinguishing gifted from accelerated students. Rather than using a standardized test to distinguish gifted students from accelerated ones, we have relied on teacher anecdotal records as a means of identifying gifted students in our Chemistry/Physics Program. The following example will illustrate how we have used anecdotal observations to identify gifted students in our program.

Three years ago, we had a student who had quickly mastered the concepts related to electromagnetism and the fact that time-dependent electric fields "turn on" magnetic fields and vice-versa. One day, after this material had just been introduced, he came to one of us and brought up the idea that something similar should happen with time-dependent gravitational fields since so much of the mathematical foundation was similar to that of electromagnetism. Because of his superior scientific insight due to concept attainment, this student was able to think in mathematically abstract terms. For this reason, he was allowing himself to develop independently the concept of gravitomagnetism that Albert Einstein had predicted. A typically accelerated student would not be able to think in such abstract terms and would not be able to apply this kind of reasoning to something so physically different, yet conceptually similar. The accelerated students are not as likely to make connections between the concepts that they have learned in class with other phenomena outside of the curriculum due to their limited scientific insight.

The Chemistry/Physics Program is a 3-year program that begins in 10th grade. This means that students enrolled in the program must be identified at the end of their freshman year. Up to about 10 years ago, the Science Department at our high school offered a course called "Life Science Honors" (LSH) in the freshman year. This course emphasized the use of the inquiry approach to teach biology to freshmen. Prospective students for the Chemistry/Physics Program were identified from this class. Success in Life Science Honors course (a grade of B or better) and success in Honors Freshman Mathematics (on track to take Calculus by the senior year) were some of the requirements that a student had to fulfill in order to be invited in the Chemistry/Physics class. Other requirements included a favorable teacher recommendation and success on the California Achievement Test (CAT). A 90th percentile or higher on the CAT was required to qualify for the program.

About 10 years ago, the freshman Life Science Honors course and the sophomore Biology Honors course were combined to produce a single Biology Honors course for the freshman year. This is the only science course that has been taught in the freshman year for the last 10 years. Placement for Biology Honors is done by teacher analysis of student skills and success on the ACT Explore Test. The chairperson of the Science Department bases his decision on student performance on all four sections of the Explore Test. He usually selects students in the top three stanines, that is, in the 77th percentile or higher.

For admission to the Chemistry/Physics program, the Science Department chairperson relies on teacher recommendations from the Biology Honors course and documented success in mathematics. Students who are strong in mathematics and who are headed to taking Calculus by their senior year are highly sought for the Chemistry/Physics Program. Lately, success in mathematics has become a stronger indicator for appropriate placement in the program.

After the students join the Chemistry/Physics Program during their sophomore year, we start to compile teacher anecdotal records on each one of them. Students who display an outstanding scientific insight are identified as gifted. We have found that it is not possible to place this label on students based on other, more objective criteria such as test scores. High scores on tests are not always indicative of a student's scientific insight. Each year, there are usually 5 to 10 students whom we identify as gifted.

Recent Changes in the Chemistry/Physics Program

When the Chemistry/Physics Program was first started in 1952, gifted students made up a larger percentage of the students in the program than we have today. This kind of student body played a major role in the decision that was taken with respect to the organization of the program. Students who were going to begin the program in grade 10 were identified by middle school teachers in grade 8, and all took Honors Biology in grade 9. The decision to teach both Chemistry and Physics Honors in one year (grade 10) was based on the fact that students would be exposed only to the major conceptual schemes in chemistry and physics and that they would then investigate details of these concepts on their own. Typical enrollment was 30 to 40 students, and all of these students went on to take the AP courses in grades 11 and 12. The majority of the students were quite mathematically advanced and would take Multivariable Calculus and Linear Algebra by their senior year.

In the past few years, however, the number of gifted students and mathematically advanced students has remained about the same, while the total enrollment in the program has increased dramatically after it was decided to open it up to all who wanted to try. All students in grade 9 now take Biology, with between 150 and 200 taking Honors Biology. For example, 2 years ago, there were nearly 120 students who took the grade 10 honors course, and about 90 went on to begin AP courses in grades 11 and 12. The teaching has also become geared toward the accelerated students who make up a larger portion of the student body. There is a danger that the gifted students would become bored with the slower pace suited for the accelerated students. In order to keep the gifted students continuously challenged, other curricular options had to be considered.

Options for the Gifted Science Student

Once we identify gifted students, we encourage them to get involved in a variety of challenging academic and research-based activities. For example, students who are advanced in mathematics may be encouraged to take more advanced mathematics classes at Northwestern University. Sometimes, students choose to carry out an independent study by developing their own course with a sponsoring teacher at the high school. For those students who are looking for an even greater challenge, we provide them with opportunities to carry out original research studies in the physical and biological sciences. Most of these research studies are conducted in our own high school laboratories. Lately, a small number of our students have also had a chance to work with some professors from Northwestern and Loyola Universities.

Types of Independent Studies

We provide gifted students in the Chemistry/Physics Program three kinds of independent studies.

Students can choose to take an entire course as an independent study and receive high school credit. If the course that a student desires to take is not offered by the high school, he or she may take the course at Northwestern University. However, a student can also elect to take the course inside the high school if a high school teacher qualified to teach the course can be found. For example, several years ago, we had two students who had taken all the advanced mathematics courses (Linear Algebra, Multivariable Calculus) our school offered. Because they wanted to take more advanced mathematics courses, they decided to take Group Theory as an independent study with one of the faculty members in the Mathematics Department.

The second type of independent study is an outgrowth of special interest that students develop in the topics discussed in our Advanced Placement Chemistry and Physics courses. In Advanced Placement Physics, for example, several gifted students usually choose to study relativity and higher-level Lagrangian mechanics in more depth simply to satisfy their intellectual curiosity. It is also not unusual to have students who choose to study quantum mechanics in more depth in Advanced Placement Chemistry. Students do not receive extra credit for this type of independent study, but this does not prevent gifted students from engaging in these intellectual endeavors. They carry out this type of independent study for the intellectual challenge it represents.

The last type of independent study involves some types of hands-on activities. This may involve laboratory or computer work or a combination of both. In Advanced Placement Chemistry, for example, students have studied oscillating reactions as an independent study. Others have used molecular modeling via computer to investigate the crystal structure of benzene. In Advanced Placement Physics, for example, students have written their own computer programs to simulate various chaotic mechanical devices and fractal generators.

From the above discussion, one can see that nurturing gifted students' intellectual prowess presents an additional challenge for the teachers. In addition to the time needed to plan for actual coursework, the teacher also needs time to plan for the independent studies offered to students. This may require 2–3 more hours of planning each week. Excellent teaching of gifted students requires total commitment on the part of the teacher.

Extracurricular Academic Competitions

We have also used extracurricular academic competitions as a motivating tool to keep our students continuously challenged. A large portion of area high schools (including ours) are involved in some kind of academic competitions where individuals and groups of students are tested on their knowledge and problem-solving abilities. Some of the more popular ones among these include the Scholastic Bowl, Mathlete Math Contest, Junior Engineering and Technical Society (JETS), Worldwide Youth in Science and Technology (WYSE), and the National Science Bowl. We have been actively involved with JETS, WYSE, and, more recently, the Science Bowl, and our more advanced students have done very well in these competitions at the regional, state, and national levels.

Our experiences have shown us that the majority of the gifted students are naturally attracted to academic competitions because they provide them with an opportunity to show how much they really know (and sometimes discover what they do not yet know). However, not all gifted students are competitive, and some do not want to get involved in a head-to-head competition with other gifted students from other high schools because they are afraid of failing for the first time in their lives.

While it is important to respect a student's choice to not participate in some academic competitions, students need to be made aware that the world outside the high school walls can be fiercely competitive and that the chances of failure at some point in their lives are real. As Rimm (1995) has suggested, children actually develop self-confidence through struggle and become achievers only if they learn to function in competition, which is a side of competitions many teachers ignore.

For gifted students who are afraid of head-to-head and individual competitions, we have used other forms of academic competitions to keep them challenged. For example, the American Association of Physics Teachers (AAPT) sponsors the Physics Bowl and Physics Olympiad competitions each year. In a similar manner, the American Chemical Society (ACS) sponsors the Chemistry Scholarship and Chemistry Olympiad competitions each year. These competitions are exam-based; therefore, students are not faced with the threat of failure present in head-to-head competitions. Rather, these are competitions that look for high levels of knowledge and strong problem-solving skills. In the case of the Physics Bowl, there are both individual and team scores with some scholarship money for the highest scores. The Chemistry and Physics Olympiads ultimately determine the U.S. Chemistry and Physics Teams that compete internationally.

Student Independent Science Research

For gifted students who want to be truly challenged, they can elect to carry out original research in the major scientific disciplines. For a long time, the results of such research were submitted to the National Westinghouse Science Talent Search and the Junior Science and Humanity Symposium (JSHS) Competitions. The Science Service in Washington, DC, administers the National Science Talent Search. The Junior Science and Humanity Symposium is a program of the U.S. Army that is locally administered by the Department of Biology at Loyola University. There are regional sites for the JSHS in almost every state. Today, the Westinghouse Corporation no longer provides funds for the National Science Talent Search Competition. The funding has been taken over by the Intel Corporation. Hence, the old National Westinghouse Science Talent Search is known today as the Intel Science Talent Search. It is regarded as the most prestigious science competition for high school seniors. A relative newcomer to the list of national science research competitions is the Siemens-Westinghouse Science and Technology Competition. Both of these competitions provide a maximum of $100,000 in scholarships for the top research report paper. The Siemens-Westinghouse Science and Technology Competition has the added feature of two-person teams who work together on science research, and the top award for a team is $90,000. With this kind of money available to top students, it has become easier to find students who are willing to allocate the large amount of time necessary to carry out a viable science research project.

All the research projects that were carried out by our students from the '50s to the late '90s were done in the high school laboratories or in the students' homes. Many of the projects made use of equipment built by the students or used computer programs they had written themselves. We truly believe that it is still possible for students to do real science in a high school laboratory in spite of limited budgets. In our humble opinion, we find it unfortunate that the various national science competitions have lately tended to favor only student research projects that were done in university laboratories. In these settings, high school students often join a research project already in progress. They usually end up missing much of the research process that takes place prior to actual research activity, particularly the development of a research question and the experimental design process. Fortunately for our high school, to date, only one of our national semifinalists in the Science Talent Search (out of nearly 180 national semifinalists Evanston has had over the years) and three semifinalists in the Siemens-Westinghouse Science Talent Search have worked with professors from Northwestern University. The topics of these projects included cancer treatments and designing biomimetic peptoids that serve as lung surfactants. Clearly, these research topics could not be carried out in a high school setting due to the sophistication of necessary equipment and funding.

In our Chemistry/Physics Program, we do not require students to carry out an original research project. Instead, teachers go into freshman and sophomore science classes to present ideas about doing science research for the Intel and Siemens-Westinghouse competitions. Interested students are then encouraged to contact the teachers. Gifted students with a strong interest in science are usually encouraged to come up with their own topics for potential research projects.

In order to help these students come up with possible areas of research, we usually make available to them papers of past research studies. We also have a list of potential research topics developed by science faculty members who comprise an advisory faculty research team that we keep on hand. Students are also encouraged to browse through this list to see if they may be interested in some of the topics for a potential research area.

After a student selects a potential topic, he or she is then paired with an appropriate high school science faculty member who has research experience. The student and faculty advisor immerse themselves in the literature to learn as much as possible about the topic, as well as previous research in that area. A specific, focused research question is then developed that will become the focal point of the research project. It then becomes the responsibility of the student to develop a research plan that includes forming a hypothesis to answer the research question; design a physical experiment, theoretical computer simulation, or both to test the hypothesis; and then perform an extensive analysis of data to reach sound conclusions. Students try to complete a report on their research experience in time for submission deadlines for various competitions. This whole process normally takes about 1 full year, and most advanced and gifted students who choose to take on this challenge begin early in grade 11, although they are encouraged to begin the process even sooner.

Each teacher who supervises science research projects in the Chemistry/Physics Program usually has one to three students under his or her supervision. Some teachers have been able to supervise up to five students, but we have found that, for an effective supervision, that is the maximum possible number. Examples of topics that have been investigated in chemistry include studies of molecular rearrangement, such as the effect of mole ratio of catalyst to substrate on the Fries Rearrangement of thymyl acetate and designing novel methods for the synthesis of selected organic compounds by the electrosynthetic method, just to name a few. In physics, studies of heat flow through materials, fluid dynamics, the properties of granular materials, and numerous other topics have helped provide a rich and diverse research program. Research studies culminate in the submission of a 20-page, double-spaced research report to the Intel Talent Search or to the Siemens-Westinghouse Science and Technology Competition.

The Science Department provides most of the materials used in the research by the students. Teachers who supervise research receive an extra stipend from the Board of Education of District 202. Our faculty research team is relatively new, as we have begun to take an approach that is modeled after university research groups. Faculty members who have research experience and are from a variety of disciplines meet regularly to discuss individual student progress, new research topics, and long-range planning for science research in the high school. Such an approach allows for a larger variety of potential projects, as well as an emphasis on the interdisciplinary nature of model science research in the real world. In addition, we have greater contact with more students who may want to pursue research and have begun to get more freshman and sophomore students involved in research, thus giving them more time to develop and refine a project before submitting it to a competition. We have recently begun a research class that freshmen can take to learn about the scientific method as well as begin to develop ideas that they may investigate in the lab over an extended period of time.

Conclusion

Because gifted students can easily and quickly master topics discussed in a typical Advanced Placement Chemistry or Physics class, there is a danger that they may become bored if other options are not utilized. At Evanston Township High School, we have used a combination of independent studies, extracurricular academic competitions, and independent science research projects to keep our gifted students in the Chemistry/Physics Program continuously challenged and motivated. Gifted students need more than standard classroom activities because these can be too easy for them. Our experience shows that gifted students appreciate a variety of additional learning activities because they have many interests that lie outside the standard AP curricula. A good majority of these students (about 90%) remain interested in science and mathematics and go on to major in these areas of study in top colleges around the country. In addition, approximately 95% of all graduates who have taken the Chemistry/Physics Program have reported in surveys that they definitely feel better prepared for college and careers not only because they had college-level material in high school, but also because of the study skills and time-management skills they developed by taking on multiple challenges that were offered outside of the standard curricula. It is imperative that we continue to challenge our best and brightest even in times when it seems there are fewer resources being allocated for them. In some cases, teachers must take it upon themselves to get these students involved in studies and activities that will allow them to take advantage of their gifts and develop into the next generation of scientific leaders.

References

Allport, G. W. (1937). *Personality: A psychological interpretation.* New York: Holt.

Conant, J. B. (1947). *On understanding science.* New Haven, CT: Yale University Press.

Jackman, W. S. (1904). *The third yearbook of the national society for the scientific study of education.* Chicago: Chicago University Press.

Kuslan, L. L., & Stone, A. H. (1968). *Teaching children science: An inquiry approach.* Belmont, CA: Wadsworth.

Rimm, S. (1995). *Why bright kids get poor grades.* New York: Crown.

Science Resources on the Internet

American Association of Physics Teachers
http://www.aapt.org

Chemistry.Org: American Chemical Society
http://www.acs.org

Intel Education: Intel Science Talent Search
http://www.intel.com/education/sts

International Embryo Transfer Society
http://www.iets.org

International Society for Horticultural Science
http://www.ishs.org

National Science Bowl
http://www.scied.science.doe.gov/nsb/default.htm

Siemans Foundation
http://www.siemens-foundation.org/competition

Worldwide Youth in Science and Engineering
http://www.engr.uiuc.edu/wyse

chapter 6

Developing Scientific Talent in Students With Special Needs

an alternative model for identification, curriculum, and assessment

by **Carolyn R. Cooper, Susan M. Baum,** *and* **Terry W. Neu**

an students with learning and attention difficulties in school actually be talented scientists in disguise? If we look to history to answer this question, we see compelling evidence that giants such as Thomas Edison, Sir Isaac Newton, and Leonardo da Vinci might have been students like this. Similar to struggling students today, they had passion, curiosity, and commitment to pursue learning, often in unconventional ways. Unlike students today, however, these school failures could opt to learn elsewhere—frequently, by themselves or with a mentor.

Today, we have multiple ways to support our student scientists. There are magnet schools, special schools in math and science, Advanced Placement courses, and honors classes that purport to provide the necessary scaffolding to actualize the talent of potential scientists. For students not achieving academically, however, these options are often not available because their talent is frequently obscured by their lack of achievement, their displays of inappropriate classroom behavior, or both. More specifically, to be accepted into these special programs, students must demonstrate superior scores on standardized tests of reading and math. Clearly, had these been requirements in Edison's day, his talent would have been neither found nor nurtured.

We know, furthermore, of some students who experience difficulties with reading and writing (areas emphasized heavily in school), but who have talents in science. Unfortunately, these students are not acknowledged for their abilities due to the restrictive criteria of test scores and grades. Therefore, Project High Hopes set out to address this critical issue: Could there be a talent development model in science that would both identify potential talent and provide a program in which reading and writing were not required for success?

A Talent Development Model

To create a model to meet these criteria we needed sound theoretical evidence concerning students with special needs and the best practices of talent development. Specifically, we needed to address these three questions: (a) How do gifted students with special needs learn? (b) How is scientific talent manifested? (c) What are the stages of talent development? The answers to these questions are given below.

How Do Gifted Students With Special Needs Learn?

Twice-exceptional students possess a duality of learning characteristics reflecting both their traits of giftedness and their difficulties with learning basic skills (Baum, Cooper, & Neu, 2001; Nielsen, 2002; Van Tassel-Baska, 1992; Weinfeld, Barnes-Robinson, Jeweler, & Shevitz, 2002). Specifically, when involved in their area of talent, they are more likely to exhibit positive learning characteristics. Conversely, while struggling in school, these students display behavior that is more problematic. Well documented in the literature (Renzulli, 1978; Tannenbaum, 1983; Van Tassel-Baska; Whitmore, 1980), the characteristics of gifted students include a propensity for advanced content, a desire to create original products, a facility with and enjoyment of abstract concepts, nonlinear learning styles, and task commitment in areas of their talent and interest. Gifted students also identify with others of similar talents and interests, and they possess a heightened sensitivity to failure or injustice.

The strength of these traits notwithstanding, these characteristics are frequently offset or complicated by deficits typically impeding the success of students with learning difficulties. The most commonly reported problems include limited reading skills, poor handwriting and spelling, difficulties with expressive language, and lack of organizational skills. In addition, these students often demonstrate an inability to focus and sustain attention, often display inappropriate social interaction, and exhibit low self-efficacy and diminished esteem (Individuals With Disabilities Education Act, 1995). Thus, any program we developed for these twice-exceptional students would need to accommodate their strengths and problem areas simultaneously. Table 6.1 lists these contradictory traits and the curricular modifications we made to help our students flourish in spite of their learning and attention problems (Baum, Cooper, & Neu, 2001).

How is Scientific Talent Manifested?

How do we transform these reluctant learners with strong science potential into actual scientists? How can we help them demonstrate their talent by thinking, feeling, and acting like practicing professionals? What are the skills scientists use in their work? What are the methods and materials they use? What probing questions do they ask? What are the concepts and principles of the discipline?

Not at all new ideas, these points were espoused by Bruner (1960), Dewey (1967), and others about the need to make a classroom a veritable laboratory for the exploration of ideas and scientific inquiry and an authentic setting for practicing science skills (Gardner, 1991; Renzulli, Leppien, & Hayes, 2000). In other words, these learners should be actively engaged in the discipline of science, not merely reading and writing about science.

The aim is to involve students in the discipline, not just in the subject matter. If I grind glass, study the refraction of light waves through it, and make a pair of spectacles,

Table 6.1. **Fundamentals of the Dually Differentiated Curriculum**

Characteristics of Gifted	Problems Associated With Special-Needs Students	Curricular Accommodations
Propensity for advanced-level content to accommodate the gift or talent	Limited skills in reading and math	Alternate means to access information
Producers of new knowledge through authentic products	Difficulty with spelling and handwriting	Alternate ways to express ideas and create products
Facility with and enjoyment of abstract concepts	Language deficits in verbal communication and conceptualization	Visual and kinesthetic experiences to convey abstract ideas concretely
Nonlinear learning styles	Poor organization	Visual organization schemes (e.g., timelines, flow charts, webbing)
Need for intellectual challenges based on individual talents and interests	Problems with sustaining attention and focus	Interest-based authentic curriculum
Need to identify with others of similar talents and interests	Inappropriate social interaction	Group identity based on talent or ability
Heightened sensitivity to failure	Low self-efficacy and esteem	Recognition for accomplishment

I am involved in the discipline of optometry; if I simply read about the process, I am involved only in the subject matter. Thus students need to conduct genuine scientific inquiry, not simply experiments with known answers. *They need to do what people involved in a discipline actually do.* (Arnold, 1982, p. 454; emphasis added)

The new national- and state-level curriculum standards emphasize this inquiry-based approach to teaching and learning science. The National Association for Gifted Children's curriculum standards (Landrum, Callahan, & Shaklee, 2001) for example, provide for inquiry-based teaching and learning in its positions on the importance of curricular differentiation as modifications of content, process, product, or learning environment, each of which is respectful of the individual differences of the students involved (Tomlinson, 1999). Another example of inquiry-based learning is the New York State Assessment Program in Grade 4, which requires students to design and conduct their own experiments and report their results.

Mindful of widespread national- and state-level reform initiatives, we needed to engage students in several domains of science as they acquired the knowledge, skills, and dispositions of scientists by participating in authentic science experiences.

What Are the Stages of Talent Development?

Talent development is a sequence of experiences leading students from novice to expert within a domain. Researchers examining this phenomenon (e.g., Bloom, 1985; Csikszentmihalyi, 1993) have found that students must first be exposed to topics and become excited about them. The second stage involves purposeful, discipline-intensive lessons from masters in the discipline through which students learn the principles, concepts, and skills of that particular discipline. The final stage of talent development is the stage at which students become more independent in their learning, that is, they become more interested and active in problem finding and seek alternate solutions to authentic problems within their field of intense interest (Bloom). It is this point at which students become creative producers. According to Renzulli (1977), the student makes a conscious shift from consumer of knowledge to producer of new knowledge. Organizing talent-development experiences to match this sequence would become a critical task for us as we helped students on their journey from novice to expert throughout the course of the project.

With these understandings as building blocks, the model we constructed consists of the three traditional elements of identification, curriculum, and assessment. What makes the model unique, however, is how we operationalized and implemented each of these components.

Project High Hopes

To test our model we designed and implemented a highly successful, research-based talent development program called Project High Hopes. Although the project served students with various talents, for the purpose of this chapter we will focus on the domains of science and engineering.

The project served 130 students in grades 5–8 at nine sites in Connecticut and Rhode Island, including six public schools, a private school for the learning disabled, and two schools for the deaf. Of the students identified, 72 (55.4%) attended a special school, 19 (14.6%) received resource room services in their school, and 39 (30%) were mainstreamed. These students were selected from the special-education population at each site and had been identified as having one or more of the following: learning disabilities, attention deficits, emotional or behavioral disorders, pervasive developmental disorders, and hearing impairments.

Stage 1: Exploration and Talent Identification

Authentic, domain-based activities during Stage 1 of the model introduced students to the domains of biological science, physical science, engineering design, and the visual and performing arts. These activities were part of the Talent Discovery Assessment Process (TDAP), a valid and reliable assessment tool (Baum, Cooper, Neu, & Owen, 1997), and served as audition sessions in which students' potential talent could surface. Use of this audition tool was based on the philosophy that the most accurate predictor of potential talent is information gleaned from observing student behavior over time when students are engaged in authentic domain-specific activities.

All students were invited to the audition activities, which took place over the course of 3 months. The activities were designed and administered by a professional or content expert (specialist) within each domain, and two observers recorded behaviors on corresponding observation sheets targeting specific behaviors associated with the domain being observed. Upon completion of each session, the observers and specialist discussed their observations and rated the students holistically, using a score of 1 to 3 to indicate a student's readiness for more advanced development in that particular talent

Table 6.2. **Domain-Specific Behaviors to Identify Student Talent in the Sciences and Engineering**

Science	Engineering
Displays curiosity by asking relevant questions.	Actively manipulates materials.
Shows considerable knowledge related to topic of session.	Tries to predict outcomes.
Actively manipulates materials.	Understands the main concepts of session's topic.
Communicates clearly the results of the project.	Product shows clarity of thought and focused plan of action.
Systematically tests hypotheses.	Puts materials together in a unique way.
Tries to predict outcomes.	Explains the logic of alternative solutions.
Represents ideas in the form of a model.	Shows problem solving by pursuing an unprompted investigation.
Finds means of overcoming obstacles in problem solving.	Observes patterns in experimentation.

area. These ratings were then recorded on the student summary form for use in the final discussion. Observers were encouraged to take notes on their observations and enter them on their note sheets. A list of behaviors for each domain appears in Table 6.2.

Stage 2: Discipline-Intensive Lessons

From the Talent Discovery Assessment Process we selected 63 middle school students for advanced study in life and physical sciences and 36 for engineering opportunities. It must be noted that some of these students were identified for talent in both domains, making for a duplicated count in several instances.

During the project's second stage, the activities focused on teaching the students the skills and methods of the discipline in which they had displayed talent. The dually differentiated curriculum (see Table 6.1) allowed the students to compensate for problematic weaknesses. Instruction in this highly personalized curriculum took the form of biweekly 90-minute lessons taught

**Table 6.3. Sample Lesson Topics
in Project High Hopes Curriculum**

Physical Science	Zoology	Botany	Engineering
Liquid surfaces	Microscopes	Carnivorous plants	Topography
Qualities of air	Predatory behavior of the hydra	Genetic variation in plants	Leonardo's wagon
Water purification	Pond organisms	Cells alive	Rocketry

by zoologists, botanists, a biological illustrator, physicists, and engineers.

The skill development curriculum was rooted in Renzulli's (1977) Enrichment Triad Model, with activities designed to elicit specific cognitive, creative, and affective (dispositional) behaviors characteristic of practicing professionals in each domain. The types of activities within each domain were advanced well beyond the actual grade level of students participating in Project High Hopes. Sample topics are listed in Table 6.3. Emphasis was on experiential learning that differed significantly from the traditional classroom setting. Reading and writing served the experience instead of becoming the experience. In-depth, firsthand involvement in the authentic skills of the discipline characterized the biweekly lessons taught by content specialists.

The deep understanding these students gained of the principles of engineering and science through the dually differentiated, highly advanced Project High Hopes curriculum led to students' achieving unprecedented success as learners, as well as a newfound respect from their peers. Authentic content and advanced skills comprised each session. For example, over the course of several engineering sessions, students were taught to use a transit (an instrument used by surveyors to measure angles) to measure the gradation of the school's auditorium. From these measurements, they first constructed a topographic map and then a scale model.

In biology, students assumed the role of scientists as they discovered what constitutes the diet of an owl. They carefully dissected owl pellets and, by referring to an anatomy chart,

As you are about to see, [this property] has a water feature. The feature has some problems. You will visit the site and be provided with the resources and information about the site. Once at the site, your group will be asked to gather information about the site and use resource people to help develop your plan for improving this water feature. Original, creative, innovative, useful solutions are encouraged. There is no one right answer to this problem. Groups will be recognized for excellence in their plans. Your group's task is as follows:

1. Identify the existing problems and future potentials of the site.
2. Review the resources.
3. Decide on additional information that you might need.
4. Brainstorm solutions to the problems.
5. Develop an action plan to fix the problems.
6. Prepare a presentation of your plan. (It is important to note that plans will be presented to a panel of people, some of whom have the authority to consider and implement your plan.)

Figure 6.1. **Introduction to pond problem to students**

Note. From "Project High Hopes Summer Institute: Curriculum for Developing Talent in Students With Special Needs," by M. Gentry and T. Neu, 1998, *Roeper Review, 20,* 291–296.

identified parts of the skeletal structure as they located them. Many of the students actually reconstructed a vole in the process. They also learned key concepts of a sustaining habitat, including the structure of the food chain and the carrying capacity necessary for a viable owl population. Comparison and contrast were used to determine important facts about what the owls had consumed, and probing questions led to higher level extrapolation, inference, and deduction.

Stage 3: Creative Production

In Stage 3, students applied skills and concepts learned in the Stage 2 advanced level lessons to solve authentic problems and create original products. To initiate this stage, we created a 1-week residential program in which 27 identified students worked in research teams to solve a genuine problem associated with the pond on the property. This problem-based experience gave these middle-schoolers a rare educational opportunity to become bona fide real-world problem solvers. The students were assigned to interdisciplinary teams of not only scientists and engineers, but also visual and performing artists, the other disciplines served by Project High Hopes. Within their teams, students collaborated on the problem, the goal of which was to produce a proposal containing a creative solution for reconstructing the pond (see Figure 6.1).

Learning took place in an advanced-level laboratory environment in which specially selected, highly qualified teacher-facilitators coached the individual research and development teams, or "companies," of students in the Creative Problem Solving process (Treffinger, 2000). When needed, content-area specialists (mentors) from the four domains (science, engineering, performing arts, and visual arts) furnished technical advice on tools, techniques, and materials used by practicing professionals in those specific domains. Both teacher-facilitators and mentors taught students to capitalize on their innate talents and strengths as they created a relevant proposal with supporting data, products, and budget considerations.

From Sunday through Wednesday morning, students on their respective teams were fully focused on the Creative Problem Solving process. Which species of animal life had once inhabited the pond? What degree of stress had the existing bridges tolerated? By Wednesday afternoon, students had begun to finalize plans for their forthcoming presentations to the board of directors and eagerly sought advice from the mentors on how to polish those presentations creatively and professionally.

At the Presentations Forum, held on the final day of the conference, each research and development company presented its proposal to a board of directors for the site. Before the board and the 300 or so adults and other students gathered for the presentations, the students introduced themselves as the professionals they had become in the course of the week's work. "I'm Joseph, and I'm the botanist in this firm," one student explained to the audience.

Each company then presented its proposed solution for reconstructing the pond by using an innovative approach reflecting the Creative Problem Solving techniques the students had been using all week. Combining artistically enhanced overhead transparencies, video clips, 3-D models, and dramatic performances, students illustrated both the deteriorating pond conditions they had analyzed and their respective groups' recommendations for correcting them. Most of the companies redesigned the existing structures; one team even built a scale model of the pond and constructed prototypes of a new bridge and dam.

Another team began its presentation by portraying the pond environment. The scientists then described why the pond was in the condition that it was, and the engineers explained their solution using the visual sketches designed by the artists. The group concluded its presentation with a return of the actors who then portrayed a clean, healthy pond environment, results that could be expected should their proposed plan be approved for implementation.

To be successful in this simulation, these students required a host of skills that all scientists and engineers use in a real-world setting. These skills involved math, communication, organization, and teamwork, areas traditionally problematic for students with special needs. In this context, students were able to focus on both applying their science talent and overcoming their individual learning difficulties.

In every aspect of the students' presentations, their integration of basic skills was evident. For example, one company had calculated the cost of implementing its proposal and included in its presentation an itemized budget, which reflected the higher level skills of comparison and contrast, forecasting, and evaluation. Likewise, basic science skills were integrated into the students' curriculum. Students applied the basic skill of classification as they learned to identify insects with the help of their science mentor. In addition, they applied the scientific method as they developed original experiments to test the effect of temperature on pond creatures.

Basic communication skills were enhanced by incorporating the use of video, a technique several companies employed. Their videos reflected thorough planning and organization, including creative photography, smoothly flowing scripts, and appropriate sound effects.

Students also learned the skills of organizing for work. Delineating tasks, sequencing logically for carrying out those tasks, determining who was responsible for each task, and deciding on the time needed to complete the tasks became a natural function of each company once they assembled for work. The challenges of solving authentic problems within a given time frame forced the students to organize their efforts efficiently, effectively, and economically.

Collaboration, too, is an important skill for students with special needs to learn. In one school, for example, two students collaborated as their company's scientists to develop the script for their presentation. One of these students used her superior verbal skills while a classmate, who was deaf, signed the message for the nonhearing members of the audience.

As students focused on their tasks over the course of the week, they frequently relinquished free time to continue working on their project. Students with few social skills bonded around similar interests and purposes. On the final day, there was no doubt in anyone's mind that each of these youngsters was highly talented. For this 1 week they seemed to have left their handicaps at home.

Maintaining the focus on creative productivity, Project High Hopes encouraged students to engage in activities in which they could continue to solve problems and develop their talents at levels commensurate with their nondisabled peers. These students, regarded by teachers and students alike as failures in grades 5 and 6, began to gain entrance into their districts' traditional gifted education programs, including advanced science.

Evidence of the Model's Success

Three compelling reasons signify that the model we created to develop scientific talent in gifted students with special needs was highly successful. First is the three-stage sequence of the model. Discipline-based audition activities in Stage 1 clearly discriminated levels of student talent. This cohort of students then participated in advanced-level, discipline-based lessons in Stage 2 to develop their talent. Finally, in Stage 3, when students were knowledgeable of and skillful with the discipline, they were able to apply their learning and understandings to the solving authentic problems.

Second, in all three stages, we paid close attention to providing experiences in which the students acted like practicing professionals. The use of authentic equipment, inquiry methods, tools, and materials that scientists and engineers employ motivated students and encouraged their active engagement over time.

The final reason for the model's success was our assumption that we needed to use dual differentiation to curriculum and instruction. This approach required the use of instructional strategies offering students access to high-end learning opportunities in ways that would circumvent their learning difficulties. How this was done is outlined below.

- During talent-development activities, reading and writing were deemphasized. Students' successes depended not on the traditional reading and discussing routines, but on authentic activities of constructing and applying knowledge within meaningful, experiential contexts.
- Instruction involved a minimum of teacher talk. Observations of the mentors or other professionals as they worked with these youngsters revealed that none of them spent much time lecturing to the students, especially at the start of an activity.
- Complex learning tasks were typically broken down into several manageable parts that culminated in a final product. Breaking the whole into smaller, doable tasks is a concept difficult to master for students with poor organizational skills (see Table 6.1).
- Clear and consistent communication regarding expectations was essential to the students' success. The mentors who experienced the least amount of difficulty with student discipline tended to be clear about their expectations. They presented to the group the activity's objective along with clear and succinct directions that specified what each student was to do to achieve the objective. Mentors also invited questions to clarify their directions and modeled each activity for those students who needed to see firsthand precisely what was being required of them. Finally, mentors explained to the students that, since the youngsters were being regarded as professionals, they were expected to act professionally. This expectation included the students' care and respect for the animals they were observing, as well as for the instruments and tools (microscopes, transits, drills) or materials (clay, wood, motors) they used in their advanced-level work.

- Nonemotional, verbal cues for behavior seemed effective in reminding students of their responsibility and accountability for professionalism.

- Incorporation of a problem-solving approach that results in creative products or discoveries motivated the students to engage actively in the curriculum. Experiential activities that promote problem solving benefited these students in three ways. First, because they were actively involved in learning, their attention span increased. Second, this approach allowed students to think and act in modes commensurate with their strengths. Last, learning that occurred in a meaningful context allowed for improved memory and transfer to novel situations.

- Alternate assessment procedures incorporating experiential activities and product-based learning were important in gauging students' achievement. Using experiential activities to communicate in lieu of the traditional reading and writing requirements enabled students to demonstrate their scientific knowledge within the contexts of problem solving and product development.

Conclusion

This model, purposely somewhat unconventional in its beliefs about learning, presents an alternative to traditional thinking about student identification, appropriate curriculum, and assessment of student achievement. First, identification relies not on test scores, but on audition activities, which constitute a "tryout" for a student to demonstrate his or her talent in a specific domain. Next, the curriculum differs from what schools generally offer in several ways: (1) its purpose is for the students to become creative producers; (2) it features a strong mentoring component that includes role-modeling and problem solving within specific domains; and (3) it provides these talented students with authentic, discovery-based, experiential, advanced-level subject matter of that domain. Finally, the alternate means of assessing student achievement focuses on a student's performance and the product he or she creates. Students are competitive, collaborative, and goal-oriented; they are able to apply problem-solving skills; and they experience a major shift in their own identity from loser to winner. In short, what this model assesses is the degree to which a student manifests scientific talent.

Although this model, which uses an alternate approach to identification, curriculum, and assessment, was designed for students with special needs, we are firmly convinced that it can be generalized to all students across all domains. Using this experience-based model may open the doors to talent development for many more students than those identified through the use of traditional criteria.

Traditional models often limit possibilities for personal growth, academic achievement, and success in life. Not only are talented students overlooked, but the curriculum offered to students who are identified represents more book learning than real-world problem solving. In short, as Renzulli (2001) has asserted, effective talent development occurs when "the mind, spirit, and values of each student are expanded and developed in an atmosphere that is enjoyable, meaningful, and challenging" (p. 21). We believe that our model of talent development fulfills this vision.

References

Arnold, J. (1982). Rhetoric and reform in middle schools. *Phi Delta Kappan, 63*, 453–456.

Baum, S., Cooper, C., & Neu, T. (2001). Dual differentiation: An approach for meeting the curricular needs of gifted students with learning disabilities. *Psychology in the Schools, 38*, 477–490.

Baum, S., Cooper, C., Neu, T., & Owen, S. V. (1997). *Evaluation of Project High Hopes* (Project R206A30159–95). Washington, DC: U.S. Department of Education.

Bloom, B. S. (1985). *Developing talent in young people.* New York: Ballantine Books.

Bruner, J. (1960). *The process of education.* New York: Vintage Books.

Csikszentmihalyi, M. (1993). *The evolving self: A psychology for the third millennium.* New York: HarperCollins.

Dewey, J. (1967). *The school and society.* Chicago: University of Chicago Press.

Dixon, J. (1983). *The spatial child.* Springfield, IL: Thomas.

Gardner, H. (1991). *The unschooled mind: How children think and how schools should teach.* New York: BasicBooks.

Gentry, M., & Neu, T. (1998). Project High Hopes summer institute: Curriculum for developing talent in students with special needs. *Roeper Review, 20,* 291–296.

Individuals With Disabilities Education Act (1995), 20 USC Section 1401 et seq.

Landrum, M. S., Callahan, C. M., & Shaklee, B. D. (Eds.). (2001). *Aiming for excellence: Annotations to the NAGC Pre-K–grade 12 gifted program standards.* Waco, TX: Prufrock Press.

Nielsen, E. (2002). Gifted students with learning disabilities: Recommendations for identification and programming. *Exceptionality, 10,* 93–111.

Renzulli, J. S. (1977). *The enrichment triad model: A guide for developing defensible programs for the gifted and talented.* Mansfield Center, CT: Creative Learning Press.

Renzulli, J. S. (1978). What makes giftedness? Re-examining a definition. *Phi Delta Kappan, 60,* 180–184, 261.

Renzulli, J. S. (2001). *Enriching curriculum for all students.* Arlington Heights, IL: Skylight Professional Development.

Renzulli, J. S., Leppien, J., & Hayes, T. (2000). *The multiple menu model: A practical guide for developing differentiated curriculum.* Mansfield Center, CT: Creative Learning Press.

Tannenbaum, A. J. (1983). *Gifted children: Psychological and educational perspectives.* New York: Macmillan.

Tomlinson, C. A. (1999). *The differentiated classroom: Responding to the needs of all learners.* Alexandria, VA: Association for Supervision and Curriculum Development.

Treffinger, D. J. (2000). *Assessing CPS performances: Practical resources for assessing and documenting creative problem solving outcomes.* Waco, TX: Prufrock Press.

VanTassel-Baska, J. (1992). *Planning effective curriculum for gifted learners.* Denver: Love.

Weinfeld, R., Barnes-Robinson, L., Jeweler, S., & Shevitz, B. (2002). Academic programs for gifted and talented/learning disabled students. *Roeper Review, 24,* 226–233.

West, T. G. (1997). *In the mind's eye: Visual thinkers, gifted people with dyslexia and other learning difficulties, computer images and the ironies of creativity.* Amherst, NY: Prometheus Books.

Whitmore, J. R. (1980). *Giftedness, conflict, and underachievement.* Boston: Allyn and Bacon.

Author Note

Project High Hopes was a Javits Act program (1993–96).

chapter 7

Science Seminar
*providing the opportunity
to go beyond traditional curricula*

by **Joan Mackin**, **Esra Macaroglu**, *and* **Kathy Russell**

he idea of a seminar dates back to the time of
Socrates and the ancient Greeks. According to
Barth (1990), teachers enjoyed participating in
seminars themselves since they learned to think
critically and analytically and could solve problems
that were important to them. Seminars are valuable
classes in higher education since students can discuss and guide their learning, and the question
arises as to why the seminar has not been used in
secondary schools.

It would seem logical that the seminar-type
course would easily adapt to the secondary curriculum and offer students an opportunity to guide
their own learning in subject areas that are relevant
to them. This type of course could easily be added
to existing science curricula or any subject matter
curriculum provided that an innovative teacher was
willing to develop the strategies that enable students to generate topics and possible investigations
in their own individual areas of interest. In addition to allowing students to become actively
involved in the learning process, a seminar course

would allow school districts to extend their present program in science beyond traditional curricula.

This chapter will describe how a seminar science class was successfully implemented in a suburban/rural Pennsylvanian school district. Junior and senior students were provided opportunities to become involved in their own learning, use creativity, and become emancipated from a limiting, structured program. The seminar course was introduced in the Avon Grove school district when many students expressed the desire to learn more about particular science principles beyond those covered in their courses. This chapter will explain how to develop a similar course in a secondary school setting and how teachers can adapt these ideas to their students' needs and extend their present curriculum.

Scheduling Consideration and Planning Activities

Science Seminar was an elective science course open to junior and senior students who had completed coursework for three science credits or intended to complete their last science requirement simultaneously with the seminar. The course allowed students to select and investigate an aspect of science that was either not offered or was an extension of material in other science courses. The traditional courses offered at Avon Grove High School were Physical Science, Biology, Chemistry, Physics, Earth Science, AP Physics, AP Chemistry, and Biology II. AP Physics and AP Chemistry courses took three semesters to complete, so the one-semester Science Seminar allowed students in those classes to schedule 2 full years of science.

Assessment of student progress was a continual process, and students helped plan the timeline for various checks on their research status. Everyone in the class participated in the assessment so that work-in-progress was evaluated by the individual, a chosen group, and, finally, by the teacher. So that students could help each other by positively critiquing work, class periods were used for small-group collaboration. By sharing or reading what they had done with other group members, students found weaknesses in either their arguments or presentation styles.

By the conclusion of the seminar, each student had completed a written research paper; shared with another class his or her research through an oral presentation; designed an investigation of a particular problem involving the chosen area of interest; completed a poster display showing the results of the investigation; and written an abstract about the area of interest. The students kept a portfolio showing improvements and accomplishments of work-in-progress. At various times during the course, conferences were used to monitor progress.

The students directed their own investigations and explored various means of finding information on aspects of the topic. They were encouraged to use community resources and libraries at neighboring colleges. An integral part of the course was determining what skills students needed in order to complete the tasks. Class periods were planned for instruction or group discussions on the identified new skills (e.g., oral presentation skills).

The seminar was a one-semester course that met for one period each day. The first time the course was offered, a research paper and oral presentation were expected each 9-week grading period. This criterion was modified because students had a better understanding of the subject matter if they completed the literature searches and written reports during the first grading period and completed experiments, practical applications, or problem identification during the second grading period. This change allowed for more in-depth research and gave students more time and flexibility to complete the requirements.

While students adapted to the flexibility and new responsibilities required by the course, the administration was concerned about the use of class time. Brainstorming activities, collaborative work sessions, library visits, and computer labs at various times were certainly different activities from what the traditional classes offered. Furthermore, because of the diverse interests of the students, the scope and sequence of the course changed each semester. However, a condensed program on computer skills was normally introduced early in the semester since students needed word-processing, database, and spreadsheet skills. Other topics that were standard throughout the course were how to write a research paper, give an oral presentation, and organize an investigation or experiment.

So they could work together effectively and help each other learn, students were introduced to cooperative learning and collaboration techniques. Class time spent brainstorming, judging others' work, reflecting on their own work, and generally helping each other proved extremely beneficial. Students gained insights that enabled them to use their own creativity, understand concepts, and improve their work and their products.

Since it was necessary for students to have access to journals and other resources, they needed to learn how to use the electronic library services of the high school, community, and college libraries. If necessary, students went to the school library during a class period to learn about Access Pennsylvania and other available services. Arrangements were made for small groups to visit the local college libraries to ask questions about the services offered there.

The basic idea of allowing the students to determine the skills necessary to complete projects comes from the Enrichment Triad model (Renzulli, 1977). Renzulli's model features three types of activities. Type I activities are general exploratory activities in which students identify their interests and what processes are necessary to complete the investigation. Type II activities include group training or process skills. The students in the class would identify which skills they needed in order to learn more about their chosen subject. The last part of the triad, Type III activities, includes the actual completion of investigations of real problems either individually or in small groups.

The New Role of the Teacher

The teacher was no longer the sole dispenser of knowledge, but rather became a facilitator, mentor, or guide in the learning process. Since the students had different knowledge bases, they sometimes acted as the instructor. As the course progressed, each student was responsible for sharing an article, video, or interesting discovery with the class. This introduced everyone's topic to everyone else in the seminar and enabled students to listen to and share different points of view. It worked out that some seminars had a common theme with different facets of the same subject being investigated, while others had diverse individual topics for investigations. The teacher took on the role of student when new subject matter was introduced by the pupils' investigations and needs, and experts were scheduled to teach any needed new skills in the classroom.

Because students' skills and research topics varied from year to year, the course required a flexible framework. Some order was achieved by scheduling specific events on certain days and designating other days for individual work or group activities. On those days, students who did not work on procedural skills could use library facilities or help others with additional brainstorming activities. In arranging class schedules, it was important to allow time for students to brainstorm, use critical thinking to select a topic, and choose some parameters for their investigations. Another important part of the course was teaching the class to develop a team approach and showing students that helping each other in positive ways helped them achieve their best results. This instruction relied on the ideas used in peer collaboration for teachers and team-building activities found in clubs and organizations as resources.

Reasonable checkpoints on completion of the course requirements' stages need to be included in a seminar. Initially, students selected time frames where progress would be checked. This specific schedule offered them guidance for completing tasks and allowed feedback and reflection at various stages of the process. These checkpoints also served as guides for students to use if they completed similar projects either for other classes or after graduation.

Community Resources and Guest Speakers

Effective use of community resources helped students during their investigations. Very often, neighboring businesses, research centers, hospitals, or museums have staff members who would enjoy being mentors for students during their investigations. Resources included Stroud Water Research Center and guests from colleges and universities who explained their research and its process to the students. Students also contacted on their own various community and governmental agencies that had relevant information about their research topics. One of the benefits that occurred from this outreach was the community became more interested in the school's program as the students found that the community was rich in resources.

Parents are also valuable resources and will often volunteer their time. One of the parents whose daughter was enrolled in the seminar volunteered to give a presentation on research he had conducted. The students enjoyed his talk and afterwards could relate their work to a real-world experience, as well as understand the scientific investigation process that occurs in the research phase of industry. This man continued to be a resource long after his child had graduated from school.

It is important to allow students to take full responsibility for their work and investigations. Sometimes, when students develop a project and seek help from someone outside the school, they do not find out why their mentor is suggesting certain methods or improvements to their investigations. Thus, it is extremely important for students to ask questions so they will understand why and how a certain phase of the project is being done like it is.

Standards and Benchmark

One of the concerns that a school district may have about implementing the seminar-type course is whether it will fit the existing school objectives, state and national standards, or both. The National Science Education Standards (National Research Council, 1996) gives the following content standards for scientific inquiry in grades 9–12:

Abilities of Scientific Inquiry

1. Identify questions and concepts that guide scientific investigations.
2. Design and conduct scientific investigations.
3. Use technology and mathematics to improve investigations and communications.
4. Formulate and revise scientific explanations and models using logic and evidence.
5. Recognize and analyze alternative explanations and models.
6. Communicate and defend a scientific argument. (pp. 175–176)

Understanding of Scientific Inquiry

1. Scientists usually inquire about how physical, living, or designed systems function.
2. Scientists conduct investigations for a wide variety of reasons. For example, they may wish to discover new aspects of the natural world, explain recently observed phenomena, or test the conclusions of prior investigations or the predictions of current theories.
3. Scientists rely on technology to enhance the gathering and manipulation of data.
4. Mathematics is essential in scientific inquiry.
5. Scientific explanations must adhere to criteria such as: a proposed explanation must be logically consistent; it must abide by the rules of evidence; it must be open to questions and possible modification; and it must be based on historical and current scientific knowledge.
6. Results of scientific inquiry—new knowledge and methods—emerge from different types of investigations and public communication among scientists. (p. 176)

The proposed goals of the seminar course were consistent with these standards. After investigating the benchmarks or "standards for science literacy" that were designed for the American Association for the Advancement of Science's Project 2061, a long-term initiative to advance literacy in science, mathematics, and technology, a similar conclusion was drawn. This program stresses a reform strategy that allows school districts to develop curricula that are more diversified than those presently used. Project 2061 also calls for development of programs that take into account those students who have interests, abilities, and ambitions that extend beyond the core studies.

Implementing the Seminar

Before they develop a new science curriculum, districts may wish to use a seminar course as an intermediate step to provide a different option for those students who have shown interest and talent in science. Whenever new courses are added to the curriculum, there are certain requirements that ensure the additions will become a part of the existing curriculum. These requirements include whether effective administrative arrangements will be made, whether curricular changes will take place, and whether staff development will be instituted.

A science seminar would fit well into an enrichment-type curriculum, or it could be considered an extension of the existing curriculum. One of the strengths of the course at Avon Grove High School was that it was an elective course open to students who could meet the requirements and who were interested in learning more about science. Research states that gifted and talented students need opportunities to interact with students of varied abilities and interests, to work both cooperatively and independently, to acquire skills, and to study substantive subject matter that is linked to the regular curriculum (Sato, 1988). The course certainly offered these features and included student interest and involvement.

However, one caution must be considered with this type of course. If budget constraints or increased enrollment occurs, a seminar course would probably become a casualty since it is not a required part of the curriculum. On the other hand, if student enrollment is low, the format may be easily adapted to an independent study program.

Assessment

The students kept portfolios of items and documents that illustrated their progress and their achievements. Review of the students' progress was ongoing and provided interaction between students, their peers, and the teacher. Students continually assessed the materials contained in the portfolios and, as they progressed in their research, added new items and documents they felt were important, improved the existing ones, or deleted others that no longer had significance.

A student's grade was determined by evaluating his or her research report, oral presentation, poster presentation, and abstract. Using predetermined criteria, students in the class also evaluated the oral presentation. The components of a good oral presentation were agreed upon by the students, and all involved knew the expectations for their presentations. The poster presentation was normally completed as part of a class session or followed the awards night program. Since many parents and students were invited to the awards night, an informal session was held in the gym after the program. Students could display their poster projects and answer questions at this time. This not only allowed members of the community and other students in the school to see the results of the students' efforts in the course, but also acted as a recruiting tool for the seminar itself.

An exit requirement for the course included an interview that indicated a student's knowledge about his or her chosen topic and about scientific investigation. If the school requires a formal exam, one containing a choice of open-ended questions on each of the topics could be used.

Conclusions

Myriad benefits were gained from adding the science seminar to the school's curriculum. Former students reported that the seminar experience and its requirements were invaluable to their preparations for college or training programs. Several students also reported that their interest in science continued after leaving high school. Oral and poster presentations motivated students not enrolled in the course to be enthusiastic about science. Students used the seminar to help them prepare for contests, scholarships, and other opportunities. Community members became willing partners in helping students gain a better understanding of various concepts and applications of scientific theories. For a teacher, the information and experiences that students shared gave new insights into various aspects of science that would not have been explored. New, rewarding, and challenging experiences occurred as the semester progressed. The reward of witnessing students sharing accomplishments and expertise with others made each experience worthwhile and caused anticipation of new adventures in the next semester.

References

Barth, R. (1990). *Improving schools from within.* San Francisco: Jossey-Bass.

National Research Council. (1996). *National science educational standards.* Washington, DC: National Academy Press.

Renzulli, J. S. (1977). *The enrichment triad model: A guide for developing defensible programs for the gifted and talented.* Mansfield Center, CT: Creative Learning Press.

Sato, I. S. (1988). Problems in the development of programs and science curriculums for students gifted/talented in areas other than science. In P. P. Brandwein & A. H. Passow (Eds.), *Gifted young in science: Potential through performance* (pp. 217–244). Washington DC: National Science Teachers Association.

chapter 8

Student-Centered Science Enrichment

a pyramid scheme that really pays off

by **Daniel J. Menelly**

eveloping authentic enrichment opportunities is a task that some classroom teachers reluctantly set aside in attempting to meet the day-to-day demands of a full-time teaching assignment. While struggling to meet the needs of my motivated middle school science students, I designed an enrichment pyramid scheme to allow students to extend their achievement in science. The results are encouraging in that they offer a manageable supplement to classroom differentiation and catalyze the independent thinking of young scientists.

Within the first weeks of class each year, certain students demonstrate a keen, sustainable interest in science that extends beyond their everyday classroom experiences. As a new teacher, I struggled to meet the needs of motivated students as their interests and aptitudes were revealed throughout the year. I met with limited success because my efforts at developing enrichment opportunities were almost exclusively teacher-centered. After an exhausting semester of planning and supervising a science enrichment program, I evaluated the outcome of my efforts and was disappointed. I wondered about the effect my extra science lessons and labs had on my motivated students, who tended to passively complete extension labs and experiments that were chiefly of my own design.

I resolved during my second year in the classroom to build on student interest in my subject and to afford my science students a greater sense of ownership of their enrichment opportunities. In September, I sought out six student volunteers to help build a Science Pyramid by piloting an after-school science program. The idea attracted students who were seeking leadership roles in science, as well as students who simply wanted to collaborate with peers on a science project. Over a school lunch one afternoon, I ran through a list of research and lab topics suitable for an enrichment lab, but I offered limited details. My students surveyed the lab equipment designated for the Science Pyramid (glassware, chemicals, and reference materials). They were interested in an experiment to link our study of chemistry to our upcoming work in thermodynamics. One student had recently seen a classic science demonstration of cold fire, where chemicals are combined at room temperature to create a purple flame. Another student offered an interesting variation: "How about the opposite? A chemical reaction that absorbs heat energy?"

One student secured a portable cold pack from the school nurse and set about researching its ingredients online. Another student dispatched herself to the library to compile a glossary of science terms that would enable a science student to understand the thermodynamics of an endothermic chemical reaction. A third examined the supplies available for student use and collaborated with two other students on a plan for their research. I resisted the temptation to corral their efforts in one direction and decided to see what structure the group imposed on its own learning.

I was encouraged to see my students adopting leadership roles that suited their individual strengths and promoted the learning of the group as a whole. For example, the most sequential thinker in the group initiated the task of articulating a plan to demonstrate for the team (and, later, their peers) that certain chemicals combine in such a way that energy is absorbed. The group rejected several variations of endothermic reactions as unfeasible, yet one involved materials we had worked with before. I challenged the students to modify the experiment to make it easily understood by their peers. "After all," I cautioned them, "you will face the task of safely sharing this lab with the next layer of our Science Pyramid." Their modifications included reducing the ratio of reactants so that small teams of students could feasibly experiment independently with the materials at hand and their data could be compared.

My students seemed to identify with the task of coaching a peer through a "serious" science lab. In the course of their work, I offered some guiding questions. What form of data is involved in your experiment? What can another student learn from this? What experimental protocol will you follow? As I adopted this more collaborative model of enrichment, I began to enjoy its development. Further, I found that students who helped pilot my first Science Pyramid captured the interest of their peers more efficiently than I could on my own. They were able to involve students who may not have elected to participate in a "teacher's" concept of a science question worth investigating on their own time and terms.

Students developing the enrichment labs often recruited information and content covered in my classes; yet, their treatment of the material was structured in ways to suit their own curiosity. Still, the tone of the Science Pyramid was purposeful and serious, and I wondered how many students would join the six students who had developed the first layer. One member of the Science Pyramid posted a sign-up sheet on the door of my classroom, and the group was encouraged to find a long list of students seeking to join them. Interestingly, students electing to participate represented a wide range of interests.

Because my role in the Science Pyramid was that of a facilitator, I was able to observe the learning of student participants in informal ways. They revealed sides of themselves I had not seen in class. One carefree and social student became more cognizant of safety factors and time considerations. I questioned the young man as we were packing away materials: "Hey, Matt, I liked the way you kept the group together today. Why were you more careful during the Science Pyramid than in class?"

"Well, Mr. Menelly," he replied, "we don't get to do this stuff very often, and I want to do it again."

Another student commented to me that developing a good Science Pyramid was hard work, but the initial planning simplified the actual experiment and improved the results—a small step toward science literacy. Students who had not developed the first layer of our Science Pyramid set about creating the next level. In class, we often closed our lessons by asking, "If you were to build part of our Science Pyramid from this lesson, what would you do?"

Gradually, students began proposing Pyramid layers by selecting activities and experiments that related in oblique and tangential ways to content covered in class. For example, when studying the phases of matter, several students proposed a modified crystallization lab. Later, when studying polymer chemistry, one student wondered aloud if Gak (a favorite toy slime) was a polymer. The question led to a layer of the Science Pyramid that involved a polymer reaction between borax and glue to produce a compound similar to that sold in toy stores. A canister of the result was stored away until spring. Then, during our study of light physics, a group of Pyramid scientists decided to color their polymer sample with nontoxic fluorescent pigment from a highlighter and irradiate the result with a black light.

The student-developed activities were more eclectic in nature than ones I would have envisioned, yet the process of selecting the best resulted in students reflecting on our learning in class, the scientific merit of proposals, and the interest of peers. In class, students began to refer to their experiences in the Science Pyramid during discussion. Some supported answers to essay questions on assessments with Pyramid data. Others incorporated their Pyramid work into the analysis of data in lab reports.

I have refined the Science Pyramid enrichment model in recent years by modulating the level of structure and materials I allocate to each Pyramid to suit student populations from year to year. It takes a fair amount of courage for a teacher to extend ownership of lesson development to students, but as a result of my adopting student-centered techniques like the Pyramid over time, my science teaching of the gifted has become more interactive and less onerous.

New teachers I have mentored tell me that it is often difficult to "give such power" to students, particularly early adolescents. My approach has been to balance the instructional styles that factor into my teaching and to listen critically to students as they learn. While many teachers falter in attempting to impose their own structure on each and every learning exchange in the classroom, others have exhausted themselves attempting to manage a classroom of loosely structured lessons and activities lacking a clear conceptual framework. Activities like the Science Pyramid foster a balance of structure and inquiry in a context that appeals to the social and academic development of motivated learners.

Science Units for Gifted Students

chapter 9

A Hands-on Approach
to Maglev for Gifted Students

by **Raymond T. Budd**

ifted students love the challenge of working with a technology so new that it's still in the experimental stages. One such technology is Magnetic Levitation, or Maglev, which has the promise of becoming the largest development in transportation since the wheel. As a matter of fact, Maglev does away with the wheel and all the problems inherent with it (friction, noise, energy use, safety, and so forth) by using magnetism to levitate a vehicle above a track and to move it from one place to another. The greatest advantage to this is the absence of friction. Since Maglev vehicles float above tracks instead of riding on wheels, the vehicles do not come into contact with the track or roadbed; thus, they eliminate friction. Transportation systems that use Maglev have been implemented in airports for ground transportation and in major metropolitan cities for light rail systems.

This chapter focuses on how on Maglev can be taught to students in grades 4–9 using hands-on activities aligned to the National Science Education Standards (National Research Council, 1996).

Existing Modes of Transportation

How was Stone Hinge constructed? How about the pyramids? The history of transportation studies how humans have moved goods, materials, and passengers for thousands of years. Although modes of transportation can vary (land transportation, air transportation, water transportation, travel in space through rocketry), the history of transportation typically begins with the wheel. As students learn how early humans reduced friction from dragging a load by placing it on a wheeled cart of some type, they identify the progressive improvements of transportation methods.

Throughout time, there have been a variety of ways in which objects have been transported. Land transportation can include discussions about dragsters, car designs, vehicle safety, go-carts and push carts, the use of small gas engines, and Maglev systems. Air transportation may encompass topics such as hovercrafts, airplane design challenges, lighter-than-air vehicles, gliders, and even the concept of aerodynamics. The ever-changing ideas of space travel allow students to explore the developments of rocketry and jet propulsion. Travel across waterways may include research on boats, sails, and water channels.

Once students identify the basic components, they will begin to see similarities and differences among the various types of transportation systems. When learning about each type of transportation, students analyze each in terms of construction and maintenance costs, spatial requirements, safety regulations, and environmental impact. Specific discussions regarding the effects of friction in existing transportation systems may focus on the wear and tear on parts and the required maintenance costs and power (through breaking, aerodynamic design, etc.), which is needed to overcome friction.

Principles of Magnetic Levitation

As students explore the principles of magnetic levitation, they identify how these concepts may be used in vehicle design. The role of magnets, electromagnets, and electrical current as used in Maglev propulsion help to solidify students' understand-

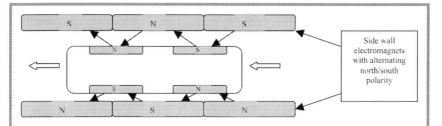

Electric current passing through a coil of wire creates an electromagnet. Reversing the current reverses the polarity of the electromagnetic. These magnets are placed in the side walls of the rail system. Permanent magnets are mounted on the sides of the vehicle. There is no motor on the vehicle itself. As the current in the electromagnets alternates, it pulls the vehicle forward. The alternating current of the electromagnets is computer-controlled for a smooth ride.

Figure 9.1. **Maglev propulsion**

ing of how the properties of attraction and repulsion result in levitation (see Figure 9.1).

During this process, the vehicle is placed on a track with alternating north and south polarity magnets. Electrical current passes through a coil of wire that touches the magnet, thus creating an electromagnet. Reversing the electrical current changes the polarity of each electromagnet.

For example, during electromagnetic suspension, magnets under the track draw on magnets attached to the body of the vehicle and propel the vehicle forward. This results in the body of the Maglev vehicle moving down the track. Electrical currents used to pull the vehicle along the track leave a constant gap between the rail and the vehicle (see Figure 9.2).

Electrodynamic suspension uses repulsion forces, rather than attraction forces. During this process, the magnets on the vehicle have the same polarity as those on the track, which forces the vehicle to float above the track (see Figure 9.3).

Advantages of Magnetic Levitation

Using model vehicles on a Maglev rack, students have the opportunity to discover the benefits of Maglev-based transportation systems. The virtual elimination of friction through

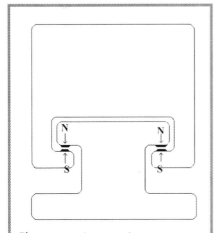

Electromagnetic suspension uses magnets mounted under the track, which draw the magnets of opposite polarity on the body of the Maglev vehicle toward them. As the magnets pull the vehicle upward, their current is electromagnetically regulated to maintain a constant gap between the rail and the vehicle.

Figure 9.2. Electromagnetic suspension (EMS)

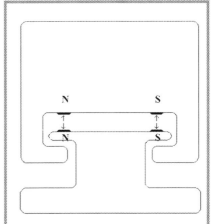

Electrodynamic suspension is based on repulsive force. The magnets in the vehicle are the same polarity as the magnets on top of the track, and the resultant repulsive force keeps the vehicle floating above the track.

Figure 9.3. Electrodynamic suspension (EDS)

the use of electromagnetic and electrodynamic suspension allows the Maglev vehicles to travel at high rates of speed and use little energy during this process. Maglev vehicles run on a unique wrap-around elevated track, which makes them safer than many rail systems because there is little chance of derailment. In addition, Maglev vehicles are comparably more quiet than existing transportation systems, and they provide a smooth, cushioned ride.

While studying existing test systems in Japan and Germany, students found that Maglev vehicles have a smaller turning radius. This means that less room is needed to change directions or turn a corner. In addition, Maglev vehicles are able to traverse more steep inclines than conventional rail systems.

When considering the environmental impacts, the Maglev system uses less energy for operation and produces little white noise (because of its reliance on electromagnetic power as opposed to internal combustion or jet engines). Video footage of the Maglev system shows a test train passing through the countryside without disturbing livestock.

Construction of a Maglev Project

When given the opportunity to design, construct, test, and evaluate their own Maglev vehicle, students decided to create a small classroom model of a Maglev transportation system. Each student made technical, to-scale blueprint drawings of his or her vehicle on graph paper (including a side, front, rear, and top view). The students shared their visions and discussed the strengths and weaknesses of each design.

Students received a kit of raw materials, including a motor, propellers, wire, straws, various pieces of wood and dowels, two pieces of Styrofoam (for the body of the vehicle), contact paper (for decoration), a plastic base (which fit the track), magnets (for the bottom of the vehicle), and Velcro (for attaching the vehicle to the base).

When considering their Maglev vehicle, students glued small magnets to the bottom of the plastic base, mounting them with the same, or like, poles facing the magnetic strips in the track. The opposing magnetic force allowed the plastic base to float above the track, and the side rails helped to maintain the vehicle's lateral position. Using sandpaper and saws, students shaped the body of the vehicle, conforming it to their blueprint designs. Using Velcro as a connection base, students were able to redesign and make modifications to both motor-powered and wind-powered vehicles. The use of colored contact paper encouraged students to be creative in the final design and decoration of their vehicle. As students tried different body types, as well as power and propulsion systems, they found that the Maglev system required the least amount of force needed to move the vehicle.

Testing and Evaluation of Vehicles

When conducting tests, students placed their vehicles on an 8-foot long and 6-inch wide track. The track had two strips of

magnets separated by a 1-inch aluminum strip. There were two L-shaped guide rails next to the magnetic strips, which kept the vehicle on the track above the strips. The two magnetic strips repulsed the base of the vehicle, providing levitation, and propulsion was provided typically by an electric motor and propeller or a sail mounted on the vehicle and a handheld hair dryer to simulate wind power.

Students were encouraged to try new, innovative techniques in their propulsion system. If they used electric power to run a small DC motor and propeller, the two guide rails were connected to a small DC train transformer and they had to devise a system of wires that would contact each guide rail to complete the circuit and supply power to the motor and propeller. This was one of the biggest problems to overcome because, when they made the wires contact the side rail, they introduced friction into the system.

Students tested their vehicles, evaluated the results, made modifications to their design and then tested the vehicles again. In most cases, the wind-powered vehicles performed better than the motorized ones due to the friction in the wiring set-up.

Helpful Hints for Presentation of Maglev Unit

Careful planning on the part of the teacher can make the Maglev unit a positive experience for students. Two areas where they may need assistance are during the cutting and sanding of the vehicle's body and in gluing parts to the body. The safety issues should be handled by teachers or by responsible students.

Individual magnets must be glued to the plastic base in each student's kit. This can be done with a hot glue gun. Students can place the magnets on the track, observing the correct polarity, and hold the magnets up for glue. Magnets should be placed as close to the edge of the plastic base as possible because anything beyond the edge would impede the movement of the base; magnet placement is critical to the operation of the vehicle. The base should be tested for smooth movement on the track before attaching the body. When gluing propellers onto the shaft of the motor, caution should be used to prevent them from flying off during the testing phase.

The body of the Maglev vehicle is constructed from a large piece of Styrofoam. This piece will have to be cut and sanded down to the shape specified in the student blueprint. This is an extremely messy task, and students invariably scatter Styrofoam bits about the room. This mess can be minimized by having the students do all cutting, sanding, and shaping inside a large cardboard box. The body of the vehicle should not be designed to extend out over the edges of the base. If a vehicle has this design, it might rub against the side rails and introduce friction into the system.

Results of the Maglev Unit

This hands-on approach to learning requires that students research, design, experiment, and problem solve. The study of Maglev technology meets the National Science Education Standards by helping students

- develop the ability to identify and state a problem (need for improvement in transportation),
- design a solution, including a risk-and-benefit analysis (design a vehicle for the project and discuss the risks and benefits of the system),

- implement a solution (construct, test, and modify the vehicle), and
- evaluate the solution (discuss the results of the experiment).

Students planned, measured, and constructed their vehicles using great care—making modifications if their test vehicle did not operate as planned. In general, those vehicles using sails and wind power performed better than those using electrical or kinetic energy. When a project was not successful, there were many opportunities to discuss potential modifications and corrections.

Depending on the time available during the day and students' ability levels, there are a variety of formats in which the Maglev concepts may be presented: multiweek periods of study, intensive weeklong projects, 1-day concentrated efforts, or hourly workshops. The discussed Maglev unit has been successfully presented to gifted students in grades 4–6 in a series of seven 45-minute sessions:

1. During the first session, students investigated various transportation systems' advantages and disadvantages.
2. The second session was an investigation, with hands-on activities and experiments, of the principles of magnetism and levitation and how they apply to the Maglev technology.

3. In session three, students discussed the advantages of Maglev over conventional transportation systems and began designing their own Maglev vehicle on graph paper.
4. During the fourth session, students completed their designs, discussed any design weaknesses with the teacher, and began construction of their test vehicle.
5/6. In sessions five and six, students completed the construction and began testing the vehicle on the Maglev track.
7. During session seven, they continued the process of testing, modification, and testing again to fine-tune the performance of their vehicle. Session seven wrapped up with a discussion and evaluation of the results of the students' experiments.

The Maglev unit has been presented in an abbreviated version for 1-day workshops for gifted students in grades 5–7. The workshops were 3 hours in length, so less time was spent on the various discussions and the design phase of the project.

If this unit were presented to older gifted students, magnetism and the experiments associated with it could be presented in much greater detail. Older students could also explore the possibility of using linear induction as a means of propulsion, rather than the more elementary systems employed by the younger students.

In all cases, the Maglev unit could and should be expanded by having students design, build, and test more than one vehicle, thus allowing them to compare different means of propulsion, as well as different body styles.

References

National Research Council. (1996). *National science education standards*. Washington, DC: National Academy Press.

Author Note

Most of the materials discussed in this chapter can be purchased from Kelvin (http://www.kelvin.com). The construction of the test track is simple with good instructions and an accompanying video. Purchase of a variable power supply from Kelvin is recommended for adequate control of motor-driven vehicles.

Maglev Resources on the Internet

Maglev Links
http://www.newton.mec.edu/brown/te/Maglev/mag-lev_links.html
Charles E. Brown Middle School maintains this site is of interesting links to other Maglev-related web sites. There are also links to downloadable Maglev-related activities, lessons, and software, as well as photographs of students testing a classroom model of a Maglev transportation systems.

The CHSST Corporation
http://www.meitetsu.co.jp/chsst/index-e.html
This Web site describes in detail a Maglev train system and includes photographs, diagrams, and technical information.

Kelvin
http://www.kelvin.com
Kelvin offers an extensive line of educational products for teaching about electronics, technology, and science. They have numerous Maglev products, including basic and advanced kits, tracks, and how-to videos.

Railway Technical Research Institute:
Maglev Research and Development
http://www.rtri.or.jp/rd/maglev/html/english/maglev_frame_E.html
This Web site contains extensive information on Maglev research and development, principles and technologies of Maglev, and test sites in Japan.

Transrapid International
http://www.transrapid.de/en/index.html
This is the Web site of the Berlin-based Transrapid International, which builds Maglev transporation systems, including one in Shanghai that has already carried more than 1 million people.

chapter 10

The Atomic Relay

integrating science and physical education

by **Daniel J. Menelly**

*t*o a science student with a basic understanding of atomic structure and electrons, the origin of visible light from within the atom is an abstract and difficult concept to comprehend. Textbooks offer two-dimensional diagrams and summaries that appeal to certain learning styles, but many science students continue to struggle with the concept.

When my science class approached a lengthy unit on the physics of light, I could see that many of my students were intimidated by the theoretical nature of the material. I started simply by asking my students to color-code a schematic diagram of an atom emitting visible light, but I had limited success in assessing their mastery of the concept. I asked another group to write a short essay, hoping that the process of translating this technical information into a language of their own would afford them a certain ownership of the idea. Again, my success was limited.

The Atomic Relay

When planning activities with my science students for a weekly activity period, I developed a plan to integrate a physical education component with our work in science class and reinforce the abstract notion that electrons emit energy in the form of visible light, a form of electromagnetic wave. In teaching science, even to gifted learners, I have found that unconventional strategies can often simplify the understanding of abstract ideas and catalyze the thinking of students with alternative learning styles. Further, they add texture to the classroom experience and build a sense of community among middle school students—a coveted goal in classroom management.

I located an orange metal basket of bright yellow tennis balls and designed an activity that might engage my students on the soccer field. I sketched a large circle and labeled electrons at its outer periphery "high-energy electrons." My students were learning that electrons in the outer shells, or energy levels surrounding the nucleus of an atom, occupy unstable high-energy states. These high-energy subatomic particles are known to shift to more stable low-energy states closer to the nucleus, giving off energy in the form of visible light in the process of switching orbitals. I created the "Atomic Relay" as a simple, concrete approach to constructing a massive human model of the atom emitting light, supplementing the teaching and reinforcement of this idea.

Students with yellow tennis balls line up along the edges of a large, loose circle about 75 yards in diameter. These students, representing "high-energy electrons," hover farthest from the atom's nucleus at high-energy orbitals. A student may volunteer to stand in the center of the large circle and represent the nucleus of the human atomic model, although a ball bearing would be more to scale. The remainder of the class gathers loosely around the "nucleus," representing electrons at stable low-energy states that hover near the atom's nucleus, attracted to the positive charges of protons there. Two are closest to the nucleus, while eight are a few yards further away at the next highest energy level. When instructed, students at the outer edge of the circle throw their tennis balls to students near the nucleus, representing the transfer of energy from unstable outer-shell electrons to stable low-energy electrons near the atom's nucleus.

Immediately after, students at the outer edge of the circle run to the center, assuming their low-energy states, waiting for a classmate to "transfer energy" (i.e., toss a tennis ball their way).

The key to the action is the pace. Middle school students tend to be a high-energy lot, and they thrive in game-like settings. I was encouraged to find my students at the inner shell calling out to outer-shell classmates, seeking an energy transfer and a chance to run to the outer part of the circle and select a classmate of their own to "promote" to a higher energy state and exchange places again. They moved quickly and randomly, as electrons orbit among energy levels within the atom.

The Atomic Relay in Action

The day before the Atomic Relay, I asked my students to wear sneakers and bring a sweatshirt to class for the activity. We mapped out the relay together on the blackboard, much like a huddle before a big game, formulating strategies and getting excited. My students were intrigued by the idea of having a science lesson outdoors, and they approached the relay with a keen sense of purpose.

"Where will I be?" one girl asked.

"You will start off as a high-energy electron at an unstable state," I replied in a serious pregame coach tone of voice.

"You mean, I'm near the outside of the atom, right?"

"That's right," another student interjected. "You throw the ball to me, and I run to the high-energy orbital. I'll look for you near the nucleus after . . ."

The day of the relay was cool and dry. Nearly every student came in sneakers. A few quickly went to their lockers for sweatshirts and light jackets. I was interested in the prerelay banter and expected to see eyes rolling, the familiar sign of indifferent teens' gentle tolerance. But, I was surprised to overhear students chattering about where they would start, checking with each other about the simple rules of the relay.

"I'm starting out at a high-energy level, so I get a tennis ball, right?" one student asked her friend.

"Yeah, throw it to me. I'm stuck near the nucleus until you do."

One student explained to his friend on the way past the front office, "It's just like a big human model of an atom giving off light. We're supposed to be the electrons."

"Oh, I get it," was the reply.

On the field, "high-energy" students lined up at the outer edges of a big circle, eyes looking sideways at their peers. I tossed a tennis ball to each student at the edge of our circle and blew a whistle. Students began tossing the balls and running back and forth, calling out to other students, running past each other as they switched orbitals.

Some of the kids were laughing, others wore serious expressions of intent, watching for tennis balls, waiting to take up "energy" and run to the outer orbitals. I let the first round go on for about 12 minutes, then gathered the class near the nucleus. I complemented them on their relay and asked students to recap the event.

"What's happening here? What's the point?" I asked.

Several students, panting, offered excellent summaries. The tone was informal, but informative, similar to the tone students use when describing the activity of a baseball game to a latecomer. After a 5-minute recap, I asked the students if they would like to run another round of the Atomic Relay.

"Yeah!"

I quickly reassigned energy states and blew the whistle for another round. After another 12 minutes, I called the class together and we returned to the classroom. At lunch, I overheard students—my students—bantering about the relay.

"Your face is red," one student in another grade commented to one of my students in the lunch line.

"I know. We ran that Atomic Relay in Mr. Menelly's class."

"But, Mr. Menelly teaches science."

"I know, but today we went outside and ran and ran . . ."

Later in the week, as part of our first light physics assessment, I asked students to explain the Atomic Relay in a short essay. "How did our class represent a model of visible light emission during the atomic relay?" Students drew sketches, labeled energy states, and relied heavily on their science vocabulary to describe the purpose of the activity. They impressed me with the seriousness of their descriptions. Several light physics labs my students performed further into the unit complemented the Atomic Relay nicely. At the end of the year, I included an extra credit question on the final exam about the Atomic Relay, and I was struck by the clarity of my students' recollections of the activity and its premise.

The next year, several of my students, then high school freshmen, returned to say "hello" and see my new classroom.

"Are your classes going to run in that Atomic Relay like we did last year?" they asked, grinning.

I told them I thought so, but that I might try something a bit different, such as asking the students to design their own relay. So far, student response to similar approaches to teaching abstract science concepts has been encouraging, and I plan to experiment more with the process as I move forward in my own learning, modifying instructional styles to suit different students as they appear each September in my science classroom.

The Atomic Relay

Objectives

1. Students use cooperation and planning skills.

2. Students gain concrete understanding of an abstract science idea through an interactive, physical activity.

3. Students build a stronger sense of community through participation as the whole group assembles a massive living model of the atom emitting visible light.

4. Students correlate the motion of a living model to the motion of subatomic particles within the atom, another model of sorts.

Alternative Activities

1. Smaller and larger groups of elementary school students can assemble for the Atomic Relay. A lesson could be team-taught with a physical education teacher, making an important link between a core subject and an allied or unified arts subject.

2. For enrichment, motivated learners can add structure to the Atomic Relay by designating concentric circles for each orbital, allowing specified numbers of peers to remain at each energy level, according to orbital theory.

3. Smaller groups could modify the Atomic Relay to involve wheel barrels and pumpkins, soccer balls, or another suitable item to represent electrons "filling up" various orbitals.

4. The Atomic Relay can be photographed or videotaped from a nearby hillside or third-story classroom and broadcast in classrooms to show the topographical image of the massive human model.

Student "directors" and "property masters" could produce the video segment and add features to dramatize its operation. For example, red crepe paper streamers could be attached to the "electrons" to show their passage among orbitals when photographed from above.

5. Velcro "energy" vests could be substituted for the tennis balls. Orbitals could becoming "changing stations." Brightly colored, easily changed vests are available in most school gymnasiums and may offer a safer alternative for younger science students.

6. Middle school science students could present their Atomic Relay to elementary science students. They may even "coach" the latter in running a relay of their own, reinforcing their own learning while affecting the learning of others.

7. Different sections of science classes may design their own versions of the Atomic Relay, comparing results with peers in different classes.

Strengths

1. Students are encouraged to view abstract ideas in science in a concrete, interactive way. Their learning is purposeful, enjoyable, and developmentally appropriate.

2. "Real physics" is demystified for students intimidated by its nature and traditional physical science pedagogy.

3. Students strengthen essential planning, design, and cooperation skills.

4. Teachers assume a collaborative role, "coaching" science students through an alternative to "pencil-and-paper" reinforcement activities.
5. The identity of science instruction is expanded.

Students are encouraged to succeed in science by making use of skills usually associated with other subject areas. An important connection is made between science, teamwork, motion, and fun.

chapter 11

~~~

Empty Lots as Modern Classrooms

*using archaeology to enrich
the gifted curriculum*

by John R. White

rchaeology is an excellent educational tool for motivating students and enriching the often routine curriculum of gifted youngsters. In several programs
(Welsh, 1994; White, 1976, 1984, 1992), gifted elementary and secondary school students have not only
studied archaeology, but have also participated as
archaeologists in "classrooms without walls."
Archaeology is an excellent curricular option because
it appeals to youngsters on multiple levels: It's intellectual, physical, invigorating, creative, healthy, roman-
tic, exciting, team-oriented, fun, and, of course, dirty.

Elementary and secondary school teachers can
begin to make use of this potentially valuable tool by
getting to know some local archaeologists. Most
schools are in reasonable proximity to a college or
university, and these institutions generally have
anthropology departments staffed with archaeologists who are often willing and eager to share archaeological procedures with interested teachers because
they realize that successful communication to and
clear understanding by the public of such important
matters as site protection and preservation create an

enlightened populace. Elementary and secondary school teachers provide an excellent network to communicate the importance and excitement of archaeology because teachers have direct and influential contact with our next generation. Once teachers have armed themselves with an ample supply of field-tested hints and precautionary notes either gleaned from written sources or received firsthand from a professional archaeologist, they can try their hand at archaeology as an authentic learning experience.

Field Archaeology

Field archaeology, as opposed to in-the-classroom archaeology, can be taught at the elementary, secondary, or university level in one of three ways: digging a genuine archaeological site, constructing and digging an artificial site or mound, or excavating an empty lot. The individual choice will largely depend on the age or grade level of the students, their experience, the pedagogical goals of the teacher, the costs involved, and the accessibility of a site.

Using a real archaeological site to instruct elementary and secondary students poses several significant problems. First, genuine sites are unique, nonrenewable resources that under no circumstances should ever be excavated with anything but the greatest care by individuals whose primary interest is the retrieval of easily lost data. While it is true that the need to instruct archaeology students at the university level does necessitate using untrained personnel to dig often valuable sites, the Society for American Archaeology ethics committee requires that instruction never be the primary reason for digging the site; rather, it must always be ancillary to accurate data removal and site preservation. Consider a parallel example from a teaching hospital. Interns are used on real operations because it is the only way they can learn to be surgeons, but their on-the-job training always takes a backseat to the welfare of the patient. Trained surgeons take over if and when the need arises. Archaeologists treat their sites with much the same deference.

Second, genuine sites cannot be counted on to provide the required scenarios needed to teach the young archaeologist properly. Many sites contain very little in the way of artifacts and subsurface features. Real sites are mostly dirt, and if the wrong one is chosen as an instructional tool, students are faced with the seemingly endless job of sifting soil. With no indication that their efforts will produce anything but minimal results, it is difficult to encourage the young and easily bored archaeologist to keep at it. In addition, teachers are unable to introduce the students to archaeological skills when the situations demanding use of those skills do not arise.

Empty Lots as Classrooms

One solution for getting around these pedagogical quandaries is to construct the site or mound from scratch and assure that it contains the required range of artifacts and archaeological problems (White, 1992). However, not everyone can afford the time and expense of constructing such an elaborate instructional device. But, there is a viable alternative: use the empty lot of a recently razed structure.

The only difference between a genuine site and an empty lot is the perceived significance of one over the other. Both are archaeological sites by definition, and the distinction lies in the fact that, in one case, there is information below ground that is in need of more careful handing than the other. Both kinds of sites must be dug with seriousness and due care. The advantage of the empty lot and the reason why it is the ideal choice for elementary and secondary students is its forgiveness of error and youthful mishap. Teachers should always check with an archaeologist to ensure that the empty lot is not a site of importance that would require professional handling.

Empty lots abound in both urban and rural areas, and one can usually be found near most schools. Urban renewal and expansion by people and businesses into the suburbs assures a steady supply of such sites. Once the site is readily available, the next task is to turn the grass or weed-covered lot into a classroom.

Designing the Educational Experience

Before you do anything else, you must get informed permission from the lot owner. Getting informed permission means telling the owner what you intend to do, and the more clearly you state your intentions, the more likely you are to get quick support. Permission usually includes assurances that you will return the property to essentially the same state it was in before you began work. Refilling holes and leveling out the ground are not only done for cosmetic purposes, but also to remove potential hazards created by the ardent diggers. Having convinced the lot owner that you will perform such corrective duties and, in the process, hinting of the favorable publicity likely to befall an individual who so generously contributes to the support of education in such a unique way, you are ready to begin converting your empty lot into a classroom.

There is a roughly sequential series of steps to be followed that are designed both to enhance the educational experience and to maximize the data recovery. Since general educational enrichment, rather than archaeological training per se or accurate information recovery, is the teacher's goal, flexibility is the rule. Thus, some of the steps may be moved about, modified, or emphasized over others.

Discuss Expectations

Like the coach with his skull sessions preceding the big football game, the teacher should spend some time discussing what might be expected once the crew is in the field. This is not so much a discussion of the physical aspects of the site (although this may be part of it) as it is an examination of what kinds of things might be found and what they might mean. In a sense, it is a defining of what archaeology is and what its potentials and limitations are.

Preparatory classroom experiments can help to frame some of these concepts. Try excavating a student's desk or, perhaps better, the teacher's wastepaper basket. Show how careful attention to the position and layering (*stratigraphy* to the archaeologist) of the various items in the basket can be interpreted to tell us things about the people responsible for filling it. Let the young imaginations soar. Caution the wildly extravagant, but, as in brainstorming sessions, do not discourage Icarus-like flights. You never know from where great ideas may come.

Form Your Working Hypotheses

Explain what is meant by a hypothesis. Go beyond merely defining it as an educated guess and explain how scientists use hypotheses to test various points of view. Hypotheses should be conceptually clear and unambiguous, related to objective and observable phenomena, simply stated, testable, plausible, and meaningful.

Once the concept is understood, make a working list of hypotheses for the site to be investigated. The following are some examples: "The specific location of various artifacts will reflect the activities carried out in each area of the site"; "The type and range of artifacts are reflective of the gender, age, and number of the population using the site"; "The thickness of the site deposit is an indication of how long the site was inhabited"; and "The age of the artifacts is a clue to the age of the site itself." The list is limited only by the imagination of the group. The examples above are, for the most part, verifiable in the archaeological record, but even those not so likely to be true are still valuable for teaching youngsters the scientific method.

Observe and Note the Physical Site Itself

Along with the artifacts and specimens retrieved from the site, archaeologists place considerable importance on the site itself. Geographical, geological, zoological, and botanical aspects of the unexplored site are important contributors to the determination of the site's use or function. You can tell a good deal about that empty lot you are digging by its surroundings. For instance, a lot surrounded on all sides by standing residences is more likely to have been a residence itself than an industrial site; one enclosed by a broad, paved parking area is more likely to have been a commercial site than a domicile.

Have the youngsters record copiously regardless of how unimportant the observations may seem. Such note taking not only strengthens the students' observational skills, but also contributes to their knowledge of botany, geology, landscaping, and architecture.

Grid the Site

The on-the-ground phase of archaeology begins with gridding the site into manageable subunits. An entire lot, or structural ground plan, is usually too big to excavate as a single unit. It must be subdivided into smaller pieces that, in turn, can be excavated efficiently by a three- or four-party team.

The gridding is actually done for two reasons. First, it is usual to have two youngsters doing the actual excavating while the other two sift the soil through wire mesh table screens. A unit much in excess of 2 x 2 meters is too large for most inexperienced youngsters to control. They seem to work better within close perimeters. Second, not only is the smaller subunit advantageous to the student, it is more archaeologically sound. The small unit gives the investigator tighter control of the excavation. Artifacts and specimens can be more accurately plotted according to their specific location within the site.

Common sense is called for in deciding on the grid layout. A lot measuring 8 meters along each side would normally be broken down into a grid with 16 arbitrary and contiguous 2 x 2 units if there were no other more logical reason to do otherwise. However, if the site consists of structural remains wherein room separations or walls are visible to the eye, then it would make more sense to use these as subunits because they reflect divisions that would give collected material a contextual meaning. In short, if real subdivisions exist, use them; if they do not, create artificial ones.

Vary the Site Jobs

Excavation of most sites using student help is a two-fold proposition. First, the site must always be dug with an eye toward the accurate retrieval of data. Dig supervisors have the responsibility of ensuring that their crew can handle the various aspects of data recovery in a scientifically acceptable manner. However, the teaching aspect is also important. At one time or another, every archaeologist faced with a tight time schedule or funding problem has to decide whether to go with the site (and put the best diggers in the most important areas) or go with the teaching (and put students into specific jobs without regard to their effectiveness because they need the educational experience).

Since the elementary and secondary school archaeological projects we envision are decidedly educational, every effort should be made to move youngsters into a wide variety of tasks. Students with exciting jobs must be asked to relinquish them after a time so that others may gain some experience. Similarly, youngsters excavating in units where the artifacts occur in great numbers should expect to take their turn in pits less densely populated. The idea is to develop in the youngsters a broad spectrum of field skills.

Hold Big-Picture Sessions

The tendency in archaeology is for participants to get a relatively narrow view of what is going on. Perspectives are narrowed as students' interests tend to focus on individual jobs. Though the moving around of individuals into different jobs does mitigate against narrow focus to some extent, it still falls short of providing the optimum overview.

To bring the young archaeologists into a more complete understanding of what is happening sitewide, to update them on discoveries taking place apart from where they are, and to give them a sense of greater participation in the site's excavation, the teacher should hold big-picture sessions. The purpose of the big-picture sessions is to discuss any new finds or methodological turns to be taken. They give the students the opportunity to see the site from the teacher's or dig director's perspective. Such sessions, held as often as warranted, go a long way toward teaching skills in synthesis while providing students with the knowledge they need to make intelligent decisions, evaluations, and judgments about the site.

Maintain Formal Field Records

Artifacts retrieved from a site are easily transported back to the classroom or laboratory for later description and analysis. Not so with the important nonartifactual data such as stratigraphy and horizontal context or the artifactual material like walls, floors, and chimneys that are too large and cumbersome to remove. These must be left in the field, and only recorded information on them is taken away. The most efficient and accurate way to do this is by recording on specially prepared forms.

Site forms are easy to design and can be custom-made to the type of site being dug. Letting the students help design the forms can also be an important part of the learning process. Site forms serve two important functions. First, their relative brevity allows the recording of a maximum amount of data in a minimum amount of time. Second, the visual form, with its slots and blanks to be filled in, constantly prods the youngster into becoming scientifically observant. A larger section labeled "Remarks" or "Comments" allows the imaginative or especially keen observer to add information not specifically required. Forms also provide structure, which is useful when entering the information into the database.

Maintain a Photo Record

The adage that a picture is worth 1,000 words is as true for archaeology as it is for anything else. Cameras serve a dual purpose on a dig. On the one hand, they are valuable tools for recording data that otherwise could not be removed from the site. Stratigraphy, site overviews, unit features, walls, and so forth are efficiently recorded with the camera. Professional archaeologists generally use both black-and-white film and 35mm slides for this purpose. Apart from its use in recording necessary site information, the camera is a handy and artful tool for capturing the vitality, action, and real excitement of the dig. Taking pictures of the students working at their various jobs helps to enhance the spirit of the endeavor.

Allowing the students a turn as official site photographer is a good idea because it offers them the opportunity to judge which features are important. In addition, the photographic aspect of the dig gives youngsters an introduction to the artistic side of archaeology. Teachers can use color slides to reach a wider audience and make the later showing of the slides with an accompanying commentary an integral part of the archaeological lesson.

Artifact Labeling and Cataloging

Digging up the artifacts is important; washing, curating, labeling, and cataloging them are equally important. Artifacts are bagged in the field, and each bag is labeled. If the individual specimens are not properly labeled according to their location in the site, their utility as tools to understanding the past is lost. Each artifact should be carefully marked in such a way that its provenance can always be specified. American professionals use a trinomial system that denotes the state, county, and site from which the artifact came, and they also use a specific in-site location designator to record the position of the artifact within the dig. These designations appear on both the bag and the individual artifacts within. This double marking is necessary because the bags themselves will ultimately be tossed away and the artifacts will be separated into various lots for different purposes.

The labeling and cataloging procedure works in the following way. Each unit has a set of bags into which all of the artifacts are placed. The typical bag label might read "33 MH 19, FS-22, Unit A-2." Each of the number/letter sets stands for a particular piece of site information. In this instance, the translation would be: the 19th site recorded in Mahoning County (the abbreviation), Ohio (the 33rd state alphabetically). FS-22 is the field specimen number, or the number given to the entire batch of artifacts coming from the same unit and level. Ultimately, this accession number goes into a catalog with all of the individual artifacts listed below it. The specific location within the site from which the artifacts came was unit A, level 2 (the second stratigraphic level excavated in unit A). Inventing their own cataloging system can provide the class a valuable learning experience.

Maintain a Repository

When excavating any site—even a seemingly empty lot—archaeologists are often surprised at the great number and variety of objects they will find. These artifacts and specimens are separated into like categories for later comparison, analysis, and description. The found materials are segregated into their natural departments, and such departmentalization requires space. For this reason, a portion of the classroom has to be set aside to establish a repository.

The most desirable repository places the artifacts in plain view at all times, readily accessible to sight and study. This keeps the idea of them in the front of students' minds and serves to jog their creative instincts. Also, the artifact visibility allows the students to show off the fruits of their efforts to classroom visitors. If space availability prohibits full-time display of the artifacts, they should be stored in strong cartons, plainly marked as to content, and readily available for artifact retrieval.

Produce a Site Report

Field archaeology is essentially destructive; once a site is dug, it cannot be dug again. There is a hard and fast rule in the practice of archaeology that all sites dug must be reported on. Since all of the recovered evidence remains initially and solely in the minds and memories of the diggers themselves, it must be put into a form useful for other interested people. For this reason, archaeologists write site reports.

Have an archaeologist provide you with a real site report to serve as a model. Most of them have ample spare copies that they would be glad to see put to good use. You will see immediately that such reports contain several modes of presentation, including graphs, charts, tables, drawings, maps, photographs, and text. Chapter headings can be used to evince the wide range of topics covered. Assign students or teams of students to the various tasks and have them work toward a cohesive and comprehensive presentation of their work. Putting together and editing this monograph will give the students experience in multiple academic skills. Perhaps as important as anything else, they will have produced, by and for themselves, a lasting memorial to their hard work and scholastic achievement. The teacher can add to this tribute by giving the school library its own copy.

Make a Museum Display for the School

When all the fieldwork is done and the digging tools are set aside for the season, it is time to present your artifactual treasures to the rest of the world. A proper exhibit highlights all aspects of the dig and has as its mainstay some of the more interesting things found. The trick is to show the items recovered in such a way that they draw the observer into the site itself. Things aren't just set out on a table with cardboard tags telling what they are; rather, they are exhibited in a manner that maximizes their impact and awes the audience.

The museum will allow your young artists to contribute colorful backdrops or dioramas for the artifacts, and the creative writers of the class can compose the description panels. Perhaps the school library can display the presentation in its glass cases, or maybe the principal will allow it to be displayed in the school foyer where a much wider audience can appreciate it.

Take the Show on the Road

There is a special thrill in sharing one's successes with others. Devise a way in which students can give a presentation or illustrated lecture to other classes or groups. Speaking knowledgeably in front of groups will hone the young archaeologists' self-confidence, and showing slides of the excavation, passing around and explaining artifacts, and answering questions will help them develop their communication skills.

Conclusion

Using these guidelines, it's easy for elementary and secondary school teachers to bring the thrills of archaeology into the gifted curriculum. Combining various disciplines from science to language arts, teachers can use archaeology to explore the art of discovery and join their gifted students in an educational endeavor guaranteed to work wonders. Take the classroom outside the four walls and see what it's like to have students awash in sunshine and learning enthusiasm. Who would have thought that an empty lot could become such an exciting classroom?

References

Welsh, C. (1994). Digging through history. *Gifted Child Today, 27*(1), 18–20.

White, J. (1976). Field archaeology in the high school curriculum. *American Secondary Education, 7*(1), 3–8.

White, J. (1984, Nov./Dec.). Archaeology camp. *G/C/T,* 2–4.

White, J. (1992). Fake mound, genuine scholarship: An exercise in field archaeology for the gifted. *Gifted Child Today, 25*(5), 2–6.

Archaeology Resources for Teachers

Brilliant, J. F., & Talalay, L. (1991). A sampling of creative initiatives. *Archaeology, 44*(1), 40–43.

Harrison, M. (1984). *Archaeology: Walney.* Fairfax, VA: Fairfax County Park Authority.

Hawkings, N. (1991). *Classroom archaeology.* Baton Rouge, LA: Division of Archaeology.

Lattimore, D. N. (1986). *Digging into the past.* Dominquez Hills, CA: Educational Heights.

McNutt, N. (1988). *Project archaeology: Saving traditions.* Longmont, CO: Sopris West.

Pena, E. (1989). *Archaeology activity pack.* Waterford: New York State Bureau of Historic Sites, Peebles Island.

Sanders, K. K. (1986). *Archaeology is more than a dig* [curriculum guide]. Tucson, AZ: Tucson Unified School District.

Shade, R. (1990). Grandma's attic: Bringing archaeology closer to home for the G/C/T student. *Gifted Child Today, 22*(3), 36–39.

Wheat, P., & Whorton, B. (1990). *Clues from the past: A resource book on archaeology.* Dallas, TX: Hendrick-Long.

White, J. R. (1998). *Hands-on archaeology: Explore the mysteries of history through science.* Waco, TX: Prufrock Press.

The Society of American Archaeology publishes a quarterly newsletter titled *Archaeology and Public Education* on the Web. It includes news, events, Web links, and field and lab opportunities. This publication can be accessed free of charge at http://www.saa.org/PubEdu/a&pe.

About the Authors

Suzanne M. Baum is a professor at the graduate school at the College of New Rochelle. Her research interests include twice-exceptional youngsters, creativity, and students at risk.

Raymond T. Budd is the publications coordinator at the Carnegie Mellon Institute for Talented Elementary Students (C-MITES).

Carolyn R. Cooper, a seasoned teacher and administrator with more than four decades of experience in the field of education, served as the administrator for Project High Hopes. Currently affiliated with the University of Connecticut's national Accelerated Schools Project, she directs Provider Center services for project schools in the greater St. Louis, MO, region.

Sarah Evans is currently an associate professor of biology at Friends University in Wichita, KS, where she teaches a variety of courses in both the Biology and Chemistry departments.

J. Christine Gould is an assistant professor of teacher education at the University of Wisconsin–Stevens Point. She is also the director of the Network for Gifted Education, which sponsors programs for high-ability children.

Frances A. Karnes is a professor of special education and director of the Frances A. Karnes Center for Gifted Studies at The University of Southern Mississippi.

Esra Macaroglu is a physics teacher and has been working at the Marmara University in Turkey.

Joan Mackin taught science at Avon Grove High School.

Karen S. Meador is an independent educational consultant who provides workshops and services for educators and school districts in the areas of gifted education, creativity, and curriculum development through her company Dreamcatcher Consulting.

Daniel J. Menelly teaches science at the United Nations International School in New York and is a research affiliate in materials science education at the Massachusetts Institute of Technology in Cambridge, MA.

Terry W. Neu is a professor at Sacred Heart University, where he teaches graduate and undergraduate courses in education. His research interests include science education and students who are gifted and talented.

Mephie Ngoi is currently a coordinator for Project EXCITE at the Center for Talent Development at Northwestern University.

Tracy L. Riley is a senior lecturer in gifted education in the Department of Learning and Teaching at Massey University in New Zealand.

Kathy Russell is a former education administrator and is currently working with elementary preservice teachers at Penn State University.

Mark Vondracek teaches Advanced Placement Physics at Evanston Township High School and serves as a research advisor for numerous students. He has also taught a variety of courses for the Center for Talent Development at Northwestern University.

Valerie Weeks is the director of the pre-K program at Wichita Friends School in Wichita, KS.

John R. White is a professor of anthropology and chair of the Department of Sociology and Anthropology at Youngstown State University. Recipient of five distinguished professor awards, he is the author of more than a hundred articles and the book *Hands-On Archaeology*.

Printed in the United States
by Baker & Taylor Publisher Services